Follow the Money

How China Bought the World

MICHAEL McCARTHY

Published by:
Trine Day LLC
PO Box 577
Walterville, OR 97489
1-800-556-2012
www.TrineDay.com
trineday@icloud.com

Library of Congress Control Number: 2023937748

McCarthy, Michael .
Follow the Money: How China Bought the World—1st ed.
p. cm.

Epub (ISBN-13) 978-1-63424-446-6
Trade Paper (ISBN-13) 978-1-63424-445-9
1. China Foreign relations Western countries. 2. China Foreign economic relations. 3. Globalization Economic aspects China. I. McCarthy, Michael II. Title

FIRST EDITION
10 9 8 7 6 5 4 3 2 1

Photos by author unless otherwise specified.

Distribution to the Trade by:
Independent Publishers Group (IPG)
814 North Franklin Street
Chicago, Illinois 60610
312.337.0747
www.ipgbook.com

Publisher's Foreword

We find your country is sixty or seventy thousand li [three li make one mile, ordinarily] from China Yet there are barbarian ships that strive to come here for trade for the purpose of making a great profit. The wealth of China is used to profit the barbarians. That is to say, the great profit made by barbarians is all taken from the rightful share of China.

By what right do they then in return use the poisonous drug to injure the Chinese people? Even though the barbarians may not necessarily intend to do us harm, yet in coveting profit to an extreme, they have no regard for injuring others. Let us ask, where is your conscience? I have heard that the smoking of opium is very strictly forbidden by your country; that is because the harm caused by opium is clearly understood. Since it is not permitted to do harm to your own country, then even less should you let it be passed on to the harm of other countries – how much less to China!

... The goods from China carried away by your country not only supply your own consumption and use, but also can be divided up and sold to other countries, producing a triple profit. Even if you do not sell opium, you still have this threefold profit. How can you bear to go further, selling products injurious to others in order to fulfill your insatiable desire?
    – Lin Zexu's "Letter of Advice to Queen Victoria" (1839)

Time passes, people die, more are born, the world goes around, but where will all of us be tomorrow? Will we continue to destroy our planet, our fellow human beings ... our future?

Do we ever learn?

For many years I have talked about secret societies and their trickery. I have publicly posited about a grouping based in the West that contrive with a complementary grouping in the East. And for about 30 years saying that "they" are working to "rule" the world through China. History is rife with the detritus of the attempts by these "clubs" to control our combined destinies. The goal is to divorce us from our institutions: our faiths, our families, our community. As George Washington in 1798, when asked about the "cabal" of the day, wrote that the Illuminati "actually had a separation of the People from their Government in view, is too evident to be questioned." *These machinations are nothing new.*

Michael McCarthy, a Canadian travel writer, found during his journeys around the world an amazing growth of Chinese influence. He also noticed that fellow Canadians, Jonathan Manthorpe and Sam Cooper and their respective books, *Claws of the Panda, Beijing's Campaign of Influence and Intimidation in Canada concerning China* and *Wilful Blindness, How a Network of Narcos, Tycoons and CCP Agents Infiltrated the West* were reporting along similar lines of what he was observing on his sojourns.

Follow the Money: How China Bought the World is a lively, little book which follows Michael on his journeys to many desired destinations around this wonderful sphere. We get to see through his eyes the rapacious changes happening, and he explains how this growth is exacerbating many of our current troubles. And Michael also presents some history behind the "miracle" of China's rise to dominance, which agrees with my understanding – the strong influence of Skull & Bones both in China's history and ongoing economic advance.

The Order of Skull & Bones has a long and storied history with China. William Huntington Russell, co-founder of Skull & Bones, was the scion of Russell & Company, which was America's largest opium smuggler (and third largest in the world), and responsible for a large amount of the opium trafficked into China in the 19th century. Many of the prominent families in in Skull & Bones made fortunes.

Skull &Bones members GHW Bush was the Second Chief of the U.S. Liaison Office to the PRC, and his brother Prescott Bush Jr. was a founding member of the U.S.-China Chamber of Commerce and Chairman of its Board, helping to set up the factories.

TrineDay is proud and honored to publish Michael McCarthy's work, *Follow the Money: How China Bought the World,* and it causes us to wonder: is our current fentanyl crisis karma from past actions?

Onward to the Utmost of Futures,
Peace,
Kris Millegan
Publisher
TrineDay
May 11, 2023

DEDICATION

This book is dedicated to all those hardworking people in North America whose jobs have been "offshored" to factory gulags and prison farms in Communist China and left without the means to support themselves and their families adequately, and those who have abandoned any dreams of a better future. It is also dedicated to those poor souls who have sadly fallen victim to addictions, whether to drugs or depression or consumerism, in order to find some sort of vague happiness in their lives.

Finally, it is also dedicated to all those in the western world who have recognized that the current social order – where North American corporate executives have increased their own salaries astronomically by lowering labor costs while empowering the Chinese Communist Party – is not sustainable and have started to look for other ways of doing business on a "level playing ground."

"Choose to be optimistic," says the Dalai Lama. "It feels better." Yes, it does. There is an old Chinese saying that a journey of a thousand miles starts with a single step. That first step has already been taken and now it is time to take action and spread the word. Kindly do so. The future depends on it.

Michael McCarthy
Vancouver, Canada
2023

NOTE ON SPELLINGS AND MILEAGE

Because I currently live in Canada, throughout this book I use the Canadian (that is, British) spelling of words. For instance, "labour" instead of the American spelling of "labor." Also, I try to keep to metric when writing about distance (i.e kilometres instead of miles). My spell check software, however, is American-made and does not always agree with me. Then there is the fact that I sometimes use made up words (humbility) or slang (nutbar). My apologies for any instances where I jump back and forth between the two systems. Hopefully I have spelled my Chinese words correctly, but who's to know?

Attributions to all sources of info have been included. The book has been fact checked thoroughly but the occasional error may sneak through so I apologize for that. All Canadians apologize as a force of habit; we are a polite bunch. However, if you happen to bump into Henry Kissinger, tell him he's a horse's ass. Look what dealing with the communists has accomplished! Otherwise, have a nice day.

CONTENTS

The Chinese Diaspora by country

Overseas Chinese population

● 2500000
● 5000000
● 7500000

Visualization of Overseas Chinese populations per country.
Danielnjoo, Creative Commons Attribution-Share Alike 4.0 International

INTRODUCTION

No drug, not even alcohol, causes the fundamental ills of society. If we're looking for the source of our troubles, we shouldn't test people for drugs, we should test them for stupidity, ignorance, greed and love of power.
— American humorist P. J. O'Rourke

The first rule of journalism, according to O'Rourke, is "never pay for your own drinks." Ha ha. The second rule of journalism, according to journalists sober enough to have an intelligent opinion, might be "start at the beginning." You see, every good story has a beginning, middle and sometimes even an end. To tell the whole story you need to back up the horse and wagon to the starting point, if you can find it.

If you are a certain age, you may remember the very real threat of nuclear war between the USA and the USSR back in the early sixties, when Nikita Krushchev thought he could sneak missiles into Cuba without anyone noticing. This came to the attention of U.S. President John F. Kennedy, who sent warships to intervene. As the motion picture *13 Days* later revealed, the world came very close to nuclear Armageddon.

If you are of that certain age, you may also have heard your mother tell you to "finish your food" at dinner. This warning usually came with the addendum: "There are starving people in Africa" (or China, India, Pakistan, depending on your mother's grasp of global geography). How and why a young child would have any interest in countries and starvation on the other side of the world is a different story altogether, but food was scarce those days for many people, even in North America

The point is that China was a poverty-stricken nation for centuries up to just one generation ago. Those of a current age may think that China has always been a prosperous society, cranking out vast amounts of consumer goods in "special economic zones" to send to western consumers keen to buy "Made in China" *stuff* simply because it is cheap. China was always a poor country during thousands of years of rule by various emperors and dynasties, and even under the rule of foreign countries in the 19th and 20th centuries (see Japan and Great Britain). When the Communist Party gained control in 1949, the country sank lower and lower into poverty. The old joke about communism is: "We pretend to work and they pretend to pay us." Communism is a fine idea in concept but it doesn't work in reality. Human nature being what it is, most people want to own or control what they have worked for.

In the case of China and its rise to global power, many journalists will agree that the story starts with the death of that jolly old mass murderer Mao Zedong, when Deng Xiaoping took control of the CCP (Chinese Communist Party) in 1978 and "instituted market reforms." This is bureaucratic jargon for allowing business people to do business, sometime referred to as "capitalism," as long as the CCP leaders maintained rigid control of the country and got credit for the resulting prosperity.

Should you listen to the wisdom of Wikipedia (never the most detailed source but it saves time doing deeper research), "the reforms carried out by Deng and his allies gradually led China away from a planned economy and Maoist ideologies, opened it up to foreign investment and technology, and introduced its vast labor force to the global market, thus turning China into one of the world's fastest-growing economies." In 2010, China overtook Japan as the world's second-largest economy by nominal GDP and in 2014 overtook the United States by becoming the world's largest economy by GDP. Posters of Mao still adorn buildings all over China, but sorry; it's Deng who deserves the credit, if that's what you call it.

Journalists whose own credit rating doesn't allow them to belly up to the bar and add to their tab and therefore must pay their own way can accept this prevailing Wiki wisdom or else must perform the full gumshoe themselves, which means trudging all the way back along the path of history to where the story of modern Chinese power truly begins, and that trail leads way past Chairman Mao and his Band of Renown. In fact, should you wish to compare the global economy today – where China acts as chief bartender and maintains control of the till – the real beginning of the story starts over 150 years ago with the Opium Wars of 1839-1860.

That conflict paved the way for the destruction of the Chinese economy of the time, a scenario that is being reversed today as the western world sends much of its money to Chinese factories to buy consumer goods on which the global economy is now precariously balanced. Not familiar with the Opium Wars? Let's back up the wheel of time even a bit further to provide full context. In the early years of the 1800s inventor James Watt finally perfected and patented the steam engine, a device on which engineers had been working for many years. By the 1850s the British Industrial Revolution had transformed Great Britain into the wealthiest country in the world. Fortunes were being made from factories cranking out products transported by rail to ports and on to ships and around the world. The huge British Naval fleet came in handy in several ways.

However, massive amounts of pollution dumped into rivers from factories had the unpleasant side effect of poisoning England's waterways. Water was no longer safe to drink. The population at large turned to beer. Children as young as age six were drinking booze in the factories where they worked, because only rich children went to school in those days. Great Britain became a nation of alcoholics. The British upper classes became alarmed. Production was being affected. They had heard rumors of a strange but healthy beverage known as chai, or tea, found only in faraway China. According to esteemed author Simon Winchester in his 1996 book *The River at the Center of the World,* the British East India Company sent a Scottish spy named Robert Fortune on a trip to China's interior on a mission to steal the secrets of tea horticulture. The Scotsman donned a disguise and headed into the Wu Si Shan hills in a bold act of corporate espionage, risking his life. He brought back the word about chai and the British became immediately interested and have been addicted to tea ever since.

Demand for tea soon became so high that the British actually ran out of ways to pay for it. The Chinese would accept only silver or gold as payment. Sorry, no barter or trade. Any market for Western goods in China was not allowed and trade laws denied foreigners any access to China's markets. This created a severe silver crisis in Europe and a huge global trade imbalance. The problem was only alleviated when the British found a product that Chinese consumers badly wanted; the highly addictive opium grown in the British colony of India.

The British harvested the drug, transported it to China, and ran the opium down Chinese throats by the use of gunboats on the Pearl and Yangtze rivers. As a result, the number of drug addicts in China greatly increased but the global trade imbalance was resolved. The Chinese leaders were very upset. A war started. The subsequent British victory, thanks to its naval power, resulted in the Treaty of Nanking (the Chinese later denounced it as "unequal") granted extraterritoriality to England including what soon became the colony of Hong Kong. The Chinese were embarrassed and have remained upset with the West ever since.

Looking a little deeper into addictions, an OpEd I published in the *Vancouver Sun* reveals most addictions require policing or government attention because of the damage done to the health of the addict and subsequently to the economy. The effects of drug addiction can be devastating, as the current opioid crisis in North America attests. However, addiction to some "safe" drugs such as marijuana, now legal in Canada and some other countries doesn't include the harsh damaging physical side effects such as heroin, alcohol, fentanyl and other "hard drugs" provide. Marijuana addicts don't even consider their addiction to the drug as an addiction. They think people who are not stoned are weird. In my own youth, I confess to such unbalanced dope-thinking myself. In retrospect, my favorite bumper sticker at the time was "I'm not as think as you stoned I am." Right on, brother!

Without a doubt North Americans have become seriously addicted to mindless materialism, advertised continually in all media as a cure for depression. Since many North Americans have no meaning in their lives other than the forlorn hope for some obscure "pursuit of happiness," they attempt to find some form of contentment through endless consumerism. Shopping has progressed from a necessity to a recreational activity to a passion to an addiction. For many, consumerism has become a way of life. The North American economy, formerly based on agriculture, then manufacturing, is now structured around consumerism. What once was Black Friday has turned into a Black Hole and a Shopping Season that runs from Thanksgiving to the middle of January, a "patriotic activity" needed to balance the books at Year End. WalMart is the new church to be attended on a regular basis where "made in China" is worshipped in the form of cheap sneakers and t-shirts made in gulags by political prisoners. The CCP, thinking back to the Opium Wars, must be laughing their heads off.

While Deng took power after the death of Mao in 1978, opening the door to controlled capitalism, one must look a tad further back to 1971, when Henry Kissinger, Secretary of State and National Security Advisor during the administration of the corrupt Tricky Dick Nixon, made a secret flight from Pakistan to Beijing to whisper in the ear of Communist officials. While America had been fighting communism for decades in Asia, first in Korea and then Vietnam, citing the "domino theory" that country after country would fall prey to the Communists if not stopped, Kissinger hinted that events might be changing.

Although the CCP under Mao was ruthlessly communist, showing no concern for human rights whatsoever and killing tens of millions of its own people through its "Great Leap Forward" and "Cultural Revolution" campaigns in order to maintain power, its economy had been destroyed in the process. Perhaps America might forget about fighting communism, whispered Kissinger. After all, there was money to be made. Plus, the American people were tired of seeing their young boys coming home from Vietnam in body bags. And, hey, communist USSR was the real enemy anyway. Maybe the United States and China could become buddies? Besides, Tricky Dick Nixon badly needed an image improvement. This was all kept secret from the American public, of course. No one knew of Kissinger's flight to Beijing until much later. However, the seed had been planted and would grow.

Due to an unending curiosity, I have traveled to nearly fifty countries around the world, either paying my own way or accepting invitations from various Tourism Bureaus in exchange for publishing travel articles in many Canadian newspapers and magazines, plus writing books and producing videos and documentaries. At first I thought only my home town of Vancouver was heavily affected by massive amounts of Chinese money poured into real estate. As you will discover in this book about Chinese wealth, right off the bat during trips to Los Angeles and Europe and even the South Seas I was astounded to discover that the Chinese were literally "buying up the planet." Billions of dollars have been invested in Vancouver alone, but that was chump change compared to what I discovered virtually every place I went. What could the total amount of Chinese wealth possibly be? Where in the world could these massive amounts of money have originated? Who made the investments? Who provided the seed money and designed the plan? I thought it might be a good idea to find out, so I put my nose to the trail.

As a journalist, for me the story of modern Chinese power started quite accidently, on a strange little island off the Chinese coast, where apparently the Cold War (which has no connection to the Opium War) was launched, on a trip sponsored by the Taiwan Tourism Bureau. I had never heard of Kinmen Island (formerly known as Quemoy), nor had I any plans to go there. Had I not visited the strange little sword factory of Maestro Wu on Kinmen I might never have stuck my nose into the mystery. Every good story has a beginning, middle, and an end, although that ending is yet to come. Perhaps it's time to look a little deeper into modern China, and how it has become a threat to start World War III. With regards to Mr. O'Rourke, that's certainly no joke at all.

FOR OFFICIAL

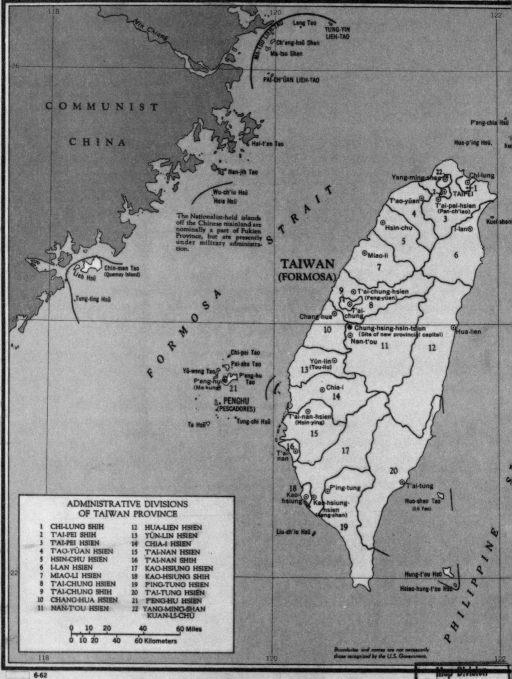

The Nationalist-held islands off the Chinese mainland are nominally a part of Fukien Province, but are presently under military administration.

ADMINISTRATIVE DIVISIONS OF TAIWAN PROVINCE

1	CHI-LUNG SHIH	12	HUA-LIEN HSIEN
2	T'AI-PEI SHIH	13	YÜN-LIN HSIEN
3	T'AI-PEI HSIEN	14	CHIA-I HSIEN
4	T'AO-YÜAN HSIEN	15	T'AI-NAN HSIEN
5	HSIN-CHU HSIEN	16	T'AI-NAN SHIH
6	I-LAN HSIEN	17	KAO-HSIUNG HSIEN
7	MIAO-LI HSIEN	18	KAO-HSIUNG SHIH
8	T'AI-CHUNG HSIEN	19	P'ING-TUNG HSIEN
9	T'AI-CHUNG SHIH	20	T'AI-TUNG HSIEN
10	CHANG-HUA HSIEN	21	P'ENG-HU HSIEN
11	NAN-T'OU HSIEN	22	YANG-MING-SHAN KUAN-LI-CHÜ

Boundaries and names are not necessarily those recognized by the U.S. Government.

6-62

585A

CHAPTER ONE

KINMEN ISLAND, TAIWAN

When plunder becomes a way of life for a group of men living together in a society, they create for themselves, in the course of time, a legal system that authorizes it, and a moral code that glorifies it."
— Frederic Bastiat

Kinmen Island off the Chinese mainland is a tourist attraction of a very different kind. Formerly known as Quemoy, there are no museums, beaches, hip restaurants, night clubs, ancient ruins or that sort of typical tourist attraction. The island is known for its tunnels. Actually, Kinmen is neither famous nor exciting but it should be. After you read this book and tell all your friends, it may well be. Kinmen has a fascinating past and an important future. It was on the cutting edge of the Cold War and if/when the CCP attempts to invade Taiwan again it may be the place where World War III erupts.

For reasons best known to itself, Kinmen belongs to Taiwan but the island is no more than a hop, skip and jump from mainland China. In 1949, the Chinese Civil War ended with the victory of the Communist People's Republic of China (PRC). The government of the Republic of China (ROC), controlled by Chiang Kai-shek and his Kuomintang (KMT) followers, along with 1.3 million anti-Communist citizens, fled from mainland China to Formosa, now known as Taiwan. Given the state of poverty in China after WWII, a lot of people joined the CCP (Chinese Communist Party) which formed the People's Liberation Army (PLA) and won a war against the Nationalists. Following Shek in grim pursuit, in 1954 Chairman Mao started an artillery barrage from the mainland aimed at destroying the General's troops based on Kinmen.

Rather than get blown to bits, the Taiwanese dug tunnels. They dug an awful lot of tunnels. They built an entire city underground, complete with streets, barracks, hospitals, schools, and even a marina. The CCP bombardment went on for years, first with artillery and then with propaganda leaflets. The Communists only gave up the battle after the U.S. 7th fleet showed up and Mao's invasion attempt ended. U.S. Secretary of State Christian Herter (1959-1961) later referred to the conflict as "the first serious nuclear crisis."

The China Quarterly Volume 62, June 1975, pages 263 to 270, contains mention of two volumes of Cultural Revolution compilations by Mao Ze-dong. Although these documents cannot be authenticated as to accuracy of transcription and are obviously selective, they throw light on the 1958 Quemoy crisis with surprisingly frank admissions of miscalculation on Mao's part, both in terms of his objective in the bombardment and his underestimation of the American response to it. However, the distinguished British historian Margaret MacMillan believes that Mao may have concluded it was in the best interest of the PLA to leave Quemoy in the hands of the Nationalists. If the PLA were to seize the islands or the Nationalists were to abandon them, the distance between the mainland and Taiwan would lengthen from a few miles to over a hundred, and lengthen "perhaps in thought as well." Moreover, the acquisition of these offshore islands by the PLA and their separation from Nationalist control in Taipei would tend to validate acceptance of the "two Chinas" policy to which both Mao and Chiang Kai-shek were vehemently opposed, both claiming to be the real boss of China.

The Taiwanese have maintained troops on Kinmen ever since. In time, they started to re-build the town above ground. Some of the tunnels were discontinued but then some genius eventually got the idea that there might be a chance to create a tourism business, somewhat like the tunnels dug by the Viet Cong in Vietnam that still draw many western tourists keen to see where "Charley" hid during the war and ate rat meat while the Yankees stuffed themselves fat with fine French food in what was then known as Saigon, now Ho Chi Minh City.

The Taiwan Tourism Bureau and I had become pleased by this time with our ongoing relationship. They had offered me complimentary trips to Taiwan several times, complete with drivers, guides and translators, to explore their country and do whatever I wanted, in exchange for my writing and publishing articles in Canadian newspapers about my experiences. In all honesty I had never heard of Kinmen Island and had not requested to go there. On this particular press trip, a Korean journalist wanted to visit Kinmen for an article he had been assigned to write. I had no idea whatsoever what we would find there,

We were guided to the entrance of a tunnel, which was guarded by a teenage boy with a goofy grin who didn't look capable of winning a wrist

A small teenage soldier "guards" the entrance to a tunnel on Kinmen Island.

wrestling contest, never mind fighting a war. We ducked our heads and entered. After crawling through a series of tunnels and establishing the obvious fact that tall people should take care for their craniums, even when wearing a hard hat, we emerged to the surface somewhat dazed but right around the corner from Maestro Wu's sword shop, a business that the Tourism Bureau also wished to promote. The front area of Maestro Wu's shop looked normal enough. There were shelves on the walls on which boxes were stacked. There was a cash register behind a counter and several smiling sales ladies, although none spoke English. The lighting was bright and modern. It looked like a simple tea shop although in this instance the products on sale were not tea, but an array of glistening metal knives and swords in various sizes. Why anyone in this day and age would want a sword as a souvenir of a visit to Taiwan I thought puzzling, but like with all good souvenirs the value is found in the back story, or the "provenance" as the word is named in regards to antiques.

We were invited past the gift shop through a set of swinging doors into the rear of the building, which suddenly transformed itself into a factory. There was a brick oven burning red from fired coal along with a row of half a dozen machines used to sand and polish metal. Throughout the room was a giant stack of what looked like old rusted metal milk bottles piled high. There were thousands of them, all loosely scattered one on top of each other in disarray. Some were standing upright, oth-

9

ers lying on their sides all over the floor. These were, we were casually informed, bombs leftover from the PLA's bombardment of the island during the Cold War. They had been gathered where they had fallen all over the island and brought to Maestro Wu's factory. It looked like he had access to enough ancient ammunition to blow up both Kinmen and the South China Sea.

Having a captive audience to witness the procedure, Maestro Wu volunteered to take a bomb and shape it into a knife right in front of our eyes. I pointed to my watch to indicate we did not have all day to stand inside a hot and smoky factory when there was still time to go find more tunnels in which we could smack our heads, but the translator responded that the Maestro could in fact create a fully finished product, from scrap metal to knife, in just over 18 minutes.

The Maestro selected a bomb from the large untidy pile. He brought it over to the furnace, picked up a pair of tongs and placed the bomb inside where it immediately started to glow. He stepped over to a foot pump and blew air into the chamber and the coals glowed even redder. After a few minutes he started to give it a good whacking with a rod. The bomb now looked like a blob. With various instruments and years of practice within 10 minutes the bomb had been reduced to the required width. He removed it from the furnace and took the blob over to a sink where he plunked it in cold water.

In less than two minutes the blob was transformed and glistened in the eerie light of the factory like a knife. When it looked just right the Maestro carried the carved steel over to a bench where he applied glue to a wooden handle and attached the steel to the handle. From start to finish the entire process took less than 20 minutes. Since they retailed at $50 U.S. a knife, I could see where Mr. Wu had acquired the name of Maestro. He had orchestrated a way to turn useless army refuse into a fortune.

All this time I had been holding my breath and biding my time, waiting for the correct moment to ask the question that seemed to be most appropriate under the conditions. Pointing to the huge stack of dusty bombs stacked on the floor, I asked the translator to inquire of the Maestro as to their condition. "How does the Maestro know these bombs are all duds? How does he know they are all safe to use?"

The translator put the question to Mr. Wu. He replied swiftly, an indication that some smartass journalist had put this question to him before. "He say they lay there on the island for many years, and after he pick them up they stay here in factory many years. They are all duds. They don't go off."

Maestro Wu fashions bombs from the Cold War into
souvenirs for tourists on Kinmen Island.

In the best spirit of contradiction for which journalists are known, I
had saved my best question for last. "What happens if and when one actually explodes?"

The question was put to the Maestro. Until this time he had not
changed his facial expression or cracked a smile. He was a serious artist
with a unique skill and a booming business. He turned to me and burst
into a big smile and said a few words to the translator. "He say if that happen," reported the translator, "then we will never know."

Should the PLA decided to invade Taiwan, at the bequest of the CCP's
current leader Xi Jinping, and nuclear weapons be used, then none of us
may ever know the outcome. For many years the CCP has been playing
a clever game now known as "soft power," where it has surreptitiously extended its range of operations worldwide, infiltrating the global economy with "made in China" goods along with an even quieter infiltration of
the political and cultural apparatus of many countries. Following a series
of well-designed 5-Year Plans since 1950, first under Chairman Mao, the
CCP under Jinping has now taken off its gloves and showed the world
its fist, and a mighty instrument it is. The Chinese government has announced its plans to retake its place on the global stage, and that desire is
to replace the United States as the world's most powerful country. Jinping

11

has stated that the days of democratic states are over, and Communism is the future. Whoever coined the phrase "domino theory" back in the day may yet be proved to be right.

According to a recent report in Al Jazeera, preparing for potential military action from China is a prospect that has hung over Taiwan since the KMT first fled to the island at the end of the Chinese Civil War in 1949. There were three close encounters between the 1950s and 1990s, and now there may be reason to worry once again as China's People's Liberation Army completes an ambitious military modernization campaign. Taiwan's Ministry of National Defense said the PLA have developed the ability to blockade Taiwan's major airports and harbors, while the Pentagon said the PLA will have the capacity to "compel Taiwan's leadership to the negotiation table" as early as 2027.

Since taking office in 2016, Taiwan President Tsai Ing-wen has focused on improving the armed forces capabilities and gone on an extensive weapons buying campaign from the United States as her government's relationship with Beijing has darkened. The administration of U.S. President Joe Biden approved a sale of $750 million U.S. in weapons to Taiwan after Donald Trump approved $5.1 billion U.S. in sales in 2020. The Taiwanese defense ministry is now asking for an extra $9 billion in arms over the next few years.

As Taiwan's horizon darkens, it needs to reckon with another big question of whether its army and the general public will be ready. Most male citizens are required to complete national service which should, in theory, prepare them to supplement the professional military, now capped at about 188,000 and rising to 215,000 if civilian contractors and trainees are factored into the equation. However, Taiwan faces serious questions about whether its reserves are capable of actually fighting successfully, like the heroic Ukrainians versus the Russians, and if an adequate system is in place to oversee them if they are mobilized in a wartime scenario. Taiwan's defense strategy has long focused on "asymmetric defense" or that it would "resist the enemy on the opposite shore, attack it at sea, destroy it in the littoral area, and annihilate it on the beachhead," according to the defense ministry. In practice, this means that while badly outnumbered by the PLA, Taiwan aims to make itself an unattractive enough target for attack by being able to carry out a prolonged resistance.

The military in Taiwan, however, has long been an unpopular career choice for young men due to low pay, poor benefits and poor social status as well as negative associations with Taiwan's previous martial law regime, when the military played a vital role in suppressing human rights. Also, Taiwan must now contend with the increasing use of "grey zone" psychological warfare and other confrontational tactics that could allow China to "seize Taiwan without a fight." These range from cyber-warfare and misinformation, to ramming Taiwanese coastguard vessels, PLA patrols of the Taiwan Strait, and sending hundreds of PLA flights into Taiwan's Air Defense Identification Zone, a swath of land and sea monitored by the military.

These patrols have multiple objectives including testing Taiwan's responses, training PLA pilots, sending warning signals to Taiwan's government, and stoking nationalism at home. Whether the U.S. would come to its defense is deliberately unclear under America's continuing policy of "strategic ambiguity" that walks the line between defending Taiwan while not angering China. Under the terms of the 1979 Taiwan Relations Act, the U.S. has pledged to "make available to Taiwan such defense articles and defense services in such quantity as may be necessary to enable Taiwan to maintain sufficient self-defense capabilities." America's guarantees, however, stop short of promising military support.

Our further media tour of Kinmen Island reveals several small villages worth having a quick look, lots of old rusting military equipment like anti-aircraft guns from the 1950s, and the Kinmen Kaoliang Liquor Factory. The company is renowned for producing high-proof distilled liquor made from fermented sorghum, fiery liquor so famous and well-liked by consumers that it has become synonymous with Kinmen. The beverage is apparently 58 percent proof liquor, similar in strength to brandy and whiskey. We reporters are told the liquor is "so potent that it has killed more people than the PLA," and we are offered free tastings, but the time of day and busy schedule prevents any malingering. Should you go, have a taste for me. You might even bring a bottle back. I will wait here for you.

THE KOREAN "WAR"

The Korean "police action" began on June 25th, 1950 when North Korea invaded South Korea. North Korea was supported by China and the Soviet Union while South Korea was supported by the United Nations, principally the United States. Cold War assumptions governed the immediate reaction of U.S. leaders, who instantly concluded that Soviet Premier Joseph Stalin had ordered the invasion as the first step in his plan for world conquest. "Communism," President Harry S. Truman argued later in his memoirs, "was acting in Korea just as Hitler, Mussolini, and the Japanese had acted ten, fifteen, and twenty years earlier."

America wanted not just to contain communism; they also wanted to prevent the so-called "domino effect." Truman was worried that if Korea fell, the next country to fall would be Japan, a country which was very important for American trade. This was probably the most important reason for America's involvement in the war. Almost 40,000 Americans died in action in Korea, and more than 100,000 were wounded. The U.S. still has nearly 30,000 troops in South Korea. The Domino Theory is still in effect.

VIETNAM WAR TIMELINE

1946 - The French Indochina War broke out with French forces largely supplied by the United States.

1950s - U.S. military advisers emerge in Vietnam in small numbers.

1954 – The Battle of Dien Bien Phu was a 57-day battle that was a complete rout for the French army. The war ended for the French shortly afterward and the 1954 Geneva Accords were signed.

1955 - President Eisenhower deploys an Advisory Group to train the Army of the Republic of Vietnam.

1961 - U.S. troops introduced on a large scale.

1965 - Active combat units were at full stage of war.

1969 - More than 500,000 U.S. military personnel were stationed in Vietnam.

1970 - Nixon announced the phased withdrawal of 150,000 troops over the next year.

1973 - U.S. combat units were withdrawn.

1975 - South Vietnam fell to a full-scale invasion by the North.

1982 - 57,939 members of U.S. armed forces who had died are listed on the Vietnam Veterans Memorial.

Chapter Two

Lotusland of the Pacific

*He who is not contented with what he has, would not be contented with
what he would like to have.*

— Socrates

You can look it up. "Beauty is in the eye of the beholder." One person's plum is another person's pits, or something like that. But in most Top Ten lists published in travel magazines, my home of Vancouver gets top marks as one of the world's most beautiful cities. At a website called *Luxury Travel Experts* Vancouver is listed as second only to Cape Town for beauty. Since I have never been to Cape Town I cannot argue. Other cities getting top marks are Venice, Paris, Amsterdam, Prague, Hong Kong, Rio de Janeiro, San Francisco, Rome, and New York. I have visited several of those cities and I would not necessarily call them all beautiful. I love San Francisco for its character although I can do without its swarms of beggars, but Vancouver is the most picturesque unless it's raining, in which case stay home, and we have enough homeless of our own, thank you very much.

Today I am playing "tourist in your own town." It's a "staycation." This story angle is sure to annoy some, who would prefer articles about some other distant destinations, but hiding within the confines of Vancouver is a secret Asian world that few tourists or even Vancouverites know about or ever visit. Sometimes referred to as Hongcouver, the suburb of Richmond is a veritable Chinese colony with its own language and culture. Its population is 215,000, of which 107,080 people or 54 percent of the City's population at the last census have a Chinese background, with that percentage growing annually with constant immigration. The city of Vancouver itself has a population of 499,000 of which 20 percent are Chinese, which is a higher percentage than the original English and Scottish colonizing population combined. Richmond, you see, represents the future.

Futurist Frank Ogden (aka "Dr. Tomorrow"), the highest paid speaker in the history of the National Speakers Bureau in Canada (whose biography I

Vancouver has experienced enormous real estate development, and cost of living, thanks to Hong Kong and Mainland China investments since the 2010 Olympics put Vancouver on the map.

wrote) used to say in his speeches: "900 million Chinese are no more likely to stay in China than the Europeans stayed in Europe." He claimed this statement always caused an uproar, with some people throwing chairs and denouncing him as a racist while he replied they didn't want to think about the future. Of all the Chinatowns in Canada or the world there is no close comparison to Richmond, and today I am enjoying a special customized tour.

My guide Mijune Pak is a well-known Chinese media personality. She is often on TV and publishes *Follow Me Foodie*, an award-winning food and restaurant guide about Chinese food, and Mijune knows everything about food and Richmond restaurants. If you want to dine on some of the best Chinese food in the world, it certainly pays to have an accomplished Chinese guide. For years I'd heard vague rumors about the Golden Village, sometimes known as the Golden Triangle. They don't all speak English there, the signs and menus are often in Chinese only, and the food is from a totally different culture. You need a guide.

Driving through the Triangle, it's impossible to see any kind of visual allure. There's nothing but ugly strip malls and endless parking lots. In reality, the Village is the second-largest Asian community in North America after San Francisco, a fascinating culture with great cuisine that rivals or betters Hong Kong. You just need to know where to find the cuisine. That's the problem. There are no maps pointing out the best restaurants and the district is hard to understand, as is the foreign culture.

The cuisine at our first stop is Cantonese. We start with rack of lamb, tiger prawns with eggplant, and pork stomach soup. Mijune relates the history of the restaurant, reveals the ingredients of each dish, and translates all my questions. Then its dim sum (brunch) at Chef Tony, hidden away in an innocuous mini-mall off No. 3 Road, high-end modern décor with several private rooms for special events. And yes, you need a reservation and you order off an iPad. The food is also Cantonese but with subtle northern Chinese inflections. Try the black truffle, pork and shrimp dumplings. Packed, fun, and friendly, it has photos of each dish on the menu, very convenient for those gweilo visitors just starting out on a journey to a foreign land without a guide.

According to Wikipedia, gweilo is a common Cantonese slur term for Westerners. In the absence of modifiers, it refers to white people and has a history of racially deprecatory and pejorative use, although it has been argued that it has since acquired a more neutral connotation. Cantonese speakers frequently use gweilo to refer to Westerners in a non-derogatory context, although whether this type of usage is offensive is disputed by both Cantonese and Westerners.

Then we drive over to fabulous Eat Street, also known as Food Street, though officially called Alexander Street on signs. There are literally hun-

Foodie blogger Mijune Pak reveals there is an entire Chinese ex-pat world in the Vancouver suburb of Richmond.

dreds of affordable restaurants in the Golden Village and over a hundred of them are located right here on three short blocks of Alexander. We slowly stroll from one end of the street to another, sticking our noses in to check menus and a quick bite. South Ocean Seafood, Strike, Thumbs Up Hot Pot, Deer Garden, Jade, Joy, Woo Fung, True's Tea House, Vivacity, Empire, Yue, Sukang, all tucked away in innocuous mini-malls. Who knew? Hong Kong-style (Cantonese) predominates in the Village, but there's also northern Chinese (Beijing, Shanghai) and southern (Szechuan), plus Taiwanese, Japanese, Thai, Korean, Filipino, Vietnamese, and Malaysian cuisines.

Many of these different cuisines can easily be found at the food courts of the four major indoor malls; Aberdeen, Parker Place, Yaohan and President's Plaza, great food at low prices, although recent inflation is another story. At Yaohan Mall I found at that time you could get rice plus four items for seven loonies (the Canadian $1 coin). On the other hand, wander over to Parker Place and you can fork out $2,080 Cdn for a tiny, 37.5-gram strip of dried fish maw. I inquire as to its culinary use and cost. Translation: "It's a very rare fish." Well, I guess so, but price doesn't appear to be a problem for many new Chinese immigrants because many seem to be rich. How they got so rich and why they don't want to stay in China are two questions I'd like to ask Mijune but she doesn't do politics.

Driving back home I decide to wander through Kerrisdale, a wealthy neighborhood formerly the haunt of British tea shops and posh English retail outlets and such; there are "for sale" signs everywhere, all of them featuring well-dressed Chinese realtors. On the main street of 41st Avenue I count over two dozen restaurants, most of them now Chinese. Watching kids pour out of prestigious Pt. Grey High School, I note most of them are Chinese. This former slice of Old Blighty has gone mostly Beijing; it's a microcosm of what is happening in much of Vancouver. Of all the cities in North America that have been the repository of newly created Chinese wealth, Vancouver is in the vanguard. What happens to Lotusland will soon be happening elsewhere. It's a great place to start to find out how the Chinese suddenly got so rich, and what the repercussions will be in the future, both economically and politically, for the rest of the world.

In 1986 Vancouver hosted a World's Fair called Expo 86. The formerly industrial lands around the inner harbor known as False Creek were turned into fairgrounds, then revitalized into a residential area known as False Creek South, which has been identified as one of the "most livable communities in the world," with its townhomes and green spaces hugging a seawall. Basically it's an urban park with people living in it. I must agree with that description because I live there myself and it is indeed paradise. False Creek North has since been transformed into a sea of shiny glass towers, but not so high as to hide the view of the North Shore Mountains.

Expo 86 fulfilled its main purpose of promoting Vancouver to the world. Chinese billionaire Li Ka-shing ("the richest man in Asia") certainly thought so. He paid $320 million for the property, but the real price is generally considered to be only $145 million, in part because the province paid the staggering cost of remediating the soil. The reality is that the government of the day made a political decision to sell the Expo lands as one single parcel to a foreign purchaser. The land could have been split up and sold as individual segments as local investors competed for the purchase, but experts agree that selling to one of Hong Kong's most highly connected businessmen sent a clear message to Asia; Vancouver was for sale, and for cheap.

In 2010 Vancouver again played host to the world with the Winter Olympics. If Expo 86 didn't draw worldwide attention, the Olympics certainly did. In 1977, the average sale price of a home in Greater Vancouver was roughly $90,000, according to the Real Estate Board of Greater Vancouver's (REBGV) chart that highlights average home sale prices from 1977 to 2017. Fast forward to 2017, the benchmark price for all property types was $1,050,300. Royal LePage predicted the median price of a Metro Vancouver detached house would increase by 2022 by as much as 12 percent to $1.893 million. In contrast, California's median home price was forecast to rise 5.2 percent to $834,400 by 2022.

For several years now Vancouver has ranked as the second-most unaffordable housing market in the world. That's according to the 16th annual Demographia International Housing Affordability Survey, which looks at middle-income housing affordability. Hong Kong topped the list for the tenth year, and Sydney, Australia came in third. Demographia rates middle-income housing affordability using what it calls the "median multiple," which is the median house price divided by the median household income. In 2020, Vancouver was given a score of 11.9, indicating the median house price is almost 12 times more than the median household income.

Andy Yan, Director of the City Program at Simon Fraser University who is often quoted in studies of Vancouver housing prices, says the ongoing challenge comes down to wage growth. Wages in Vancouver have grown a little bit but nowhere close to the kind of gains seen in terms of housing values and increases in rents. The provincial government has made legislative changes in an effort to ease the inflated market with the introduction of a Foreign Buyers Tax and the Empty Homes Tax, but will Vancouver ever become affordable to the ordinary Joes and Janes? Yan says the generally accepted rating for "affordable" is when house prices are within three to five times that of household income but for Vancouver to reach that goal either there will be a need to double household incomes, or have housing prices drop by half.

Developers insist, of course, that the only solution to the housing crisis is to further densify the city, and build far more high rise towers and town home complexes. However, driving around Vancouver for the past decade anyone will run into constant detours and stoppages because of the incredible number of construction projects already underway, from huge metropolitan complexes comprised of dozens of towers to vast new suburban neighborhoods stretching out into the Fraser Valley.

A study published by Oxford Economics in its Housing Affordability Indices (HAIs) finds that affordability deteriorated in nearly all U.S. and Canadian cities in the second quarter of 2021 as home price inflation outpaced income growth, particularly metropolitan areas along the Pacific. Authors of the report note that a typical Canadian home costs 35 percent more than the borrowing capacity of median income households. Vancouver was the least affordable of all North American housing markets, while housing continues to be more affordable in the U.S. than Canada. All across the country, eight of nine Canadian cities saw affordability decrease. Montreal was second worst, followed by Toronto, Ottawa fourth while Hamilton (southern Ontario) rounded out the top five. The report indicates that affordability will also worsen more quickly in Canada than in the U.S., largely reflecting higher Canadian mortgage rates.

Think tanks Urban Reform Institute and Frontier Centre for Public Policy evaluated housing markets for 92 metropolitan areas in eight countries to see how affordable they are. Home prices are soaring in many markets, fueled in part by investment money, low interest rates, changes in home-buying patterns, and lower inventory in many areas. 92 markets were evaluated in eight countries: Australia, Canada, China (Hong Kong only), Ireland, New Zealand, Singapore, United Kingdom, and the United States. Of those eight countries, only the United States had metropolitan areas in the affordable housing range. In the moderately affordable range were Canada, the United Kingdom, and the United States. The other five countries analyzed only had metropolitan housing markets in the unaffordable ranges.

London, the capital and largest city in England, is the world's eleventh most expensive housing market. The median house costs 8.6 times the median income. Los Angeles, California, is the tenth most expensive. The median multiple to buy a house in the Los Angeles area is 8.9 times the median income. Hawaii's housing market has continued to rise. The median multiple to buy a house in Honolulu is 9.1 times the median income. The Hawaii Realtors Association Report showed that the median housing price for the island of Oahu is now $917,500 for a single family home. Overall, single family home prices for Hawaii have risen 20 percent annually.

The tech driven Bay Area continues to be a hotspot for housing prices. It now costs 9.6 times the median income to buy a house in San Francisco, the most densely populated city in the United States. San Jose in the southern Bay Area ties with San Francisco for the eighth most expensive housing market on the list. The median house price costs 9.6 times the median income in the area. Melbourne, Australia, the second most populous city in Australia after Sydney, is the sixth most expensive housing market, with housing prices rising 16 percent.

In Toronto it takes 9.9 times the median income to buy a median house. House sales were up 97 percent from 2020, driving prices up an average of 21.6 percent. Buying a median priced house in Auckland, New Zealand now costs ten times the median income, with an average price of $1,048,000 NZD. Sydney is Australia's largest regional housing market. Buying a median priced house costs 11.8 times the median income. Vancouver is the second most unaffordable city. For the 11th year in a row, Hong Kong tops the list as the least affordable city in terms of housing prices. A median house would cost something over 20 times the median income.

Coming closer to home in False Creek, I try to find a route to get me past Broadway, a major street. It has been ripped up for over several kilometres east to west for construction of a new subway line. The Broadway Plan, as named by City Hall, will increase the population along this line by 50,000 people, mostly in high rise towers. Hundreds of MURBs, old fashioned affordable low rise apartment buildings, are scheduled for the wrecking ball. Other large swaths of the city are scheduled for sky-high development as well, such as Oakridge Centre, the Heather Lands, Jericho, Senakw at False Creek South, UBC and more. One certainly has to wonder where all the money will come from to buy these new and expensive properties, and who can possibly afford to pay the freight. For that answer, you need to travel the world and stick your nose in where it might not be wanted.

PIERRE ELLIOT TRUDEAU

Canada's national newspaper The *Globe and Mail* reports, in a history of Canadian involvement with China, that former Prime Minister Pierre Trudeau first went to China in 1949 and returned in 1960, at the invitation of the Chinese government, for a month-long tour he and co-author Jacques Hébert recounted in a book, *Two Innocents in Red China*, that was once required reading for Chinese diplomats ahead of Pierre Trudeau visits. *Two innocents* is certainly the perfect title.

The duo describes their visits to a Railway Ministry sleeping-car factory and an agricultural commune. At the latter, they watched workers smelting pig iron to fashion agricultural implements. What they had witnessed was a small part of perhaps the most grievous chapter of Communist Party history, the Great Leap Forward, which forced farmers to produce steel rather than tend their crops, resulting in a famine that killed tens of millions. What Mr. Trudeau and Mr. Hébert concluded, though, was: "We are convinced that we are witnessing the beginning of an industrial revolution."

Let's contrast that report with one by investigative reporter Terry Glavin in the *National Post* in 2017. "Canada has lately become notoriously and uniquely supine among the G7 countries in its dealings with the increasingly bellicose and tyrannical regime in Beijing, and with Prime Minister Justin Trudeau again jetting off to China, the usual background noise of humbug, half-truth and outright lies will be at full volume. It is very much an open question whether there is something either preposterously naive or scandalous and sinister underlying the Trudeau government's unseemly enthusiasm for the Chinese Communist Party leadership."

Preposterously naïve? Well, yes. As Glavin wrote, Prime Minister Trudeau himself has said that "a strong relationship with China is essential to creating jobs, strengthening the middle class, and growing the Canadian economy." Glavin says this is "the kind of boilerplate that anyone should be capable of recognizing as hogwash on methamphetamines." He reports that Canada's annual exports to China amount to a mere $20 billion. That needs to be compared to the nearly $300 billion worth of trade we send to the United States, our first-place trading partner, around $280 billion. This needs to be compared to the $66 billion in sweatshop products Canada imports from China. These numbers come from the "absurdly pro-Beijing" Asia Pacific Foundation of Canada.

The characterization of China as Canada's "second largest" trading partner is a kind of popular fiction," because you'd have to wholly ignore

Europe. Canada's new free trade deal with the European Union has already surpassed the $100 billion mark. Of course trade with Europe is governed by environmental and labour standards. Such concepts are entirely absent in China's wage-slave economy, and let's not forget the pollution.

Glavin certainly has the numbers. Ottawa's Centre for the Study of Living Standards calculates that at least 150,000 Canadian jobs were lost to Chinese imports during the first decade of this century, and at least 100,000 of those jobs were in manufacturing. But where does the Chinese wealth go? To the rich, of course. If China's wealth were spread evenly throughout its population of 1.3 billion, according to the International Monetary Fund the Chinese people would still be poorer than the people of Equatorial Guinea and only slightly wealthier than the people of Botswana."

Glavin concludes: "The 1958 to 1962 Great Leap Forward was a vast crime against humanity that Justin's father Pierre strangely failed to even notice at the time, while he was touring the country and swanning around with China's elites." The CCP elites of today have amassed fortunes for themselves equal to the GDP of Sweden. They have the money, the guns, the technology, the numbers, the UN votes, the lot. And now Beijing is openly and explicitly waging an ideological global war against democracy, the rule of law, free speech, the 'rules based' global economic order, the whole schmeer. They're quite candid about it, too."

"Even worse, you can look back over the past 30 years," he concludes "and all of the shiny forecasts about trade with China, every premise of every policy, all of it, has been wrong. The Chrétien-Trudeau Liberal grandees have not been right once in 30 years. Not once. You want to believe them now?"

The American establishment used to look askance at Trudeau the Senior, regarding him as certainly a socialist and maybe even a communist. His book *Two Innocents* manages to convey the impression that he was duped. How his son Justin has somehow managed to be duped about Chinese duplicity may be due not to innocence, but the vast profits being made by certain Canadian exporters who seem to have the Liberal Party's ear. It needs to be repeated that "if you sup with the devil you'd better have a very long spoon."

View of Downtown Los Angeles, California at Night.
Steve Jurvetson, Creative Commons Attribution 2.0 Generic

CHAPTER THREE

THE CITY OF ANGELS

Capitalism is the extraordinary belief that the nastiest of men for the nastiest of motives will somehow work together for the benefit of all.
                                                                            - John Maynard Keynes

My journey of discovery of the "new L.A." starts, of all places, at the corner of South Figueroa Street and West 9th in downtown Los Angeles. I'm staying at the Marriott Residence Inn, just across from the L.A. Live Plaza and the Staples Arena, the heart of the new downtown. Normally whenever I am visiting L.A. on a press trip I stay in West Hollywood or Beverly Hills, maybe at the Hilton. In the past nobody visiting L.A. stayed downtown because it was a dump, but I've heard rumours that good things have been happening downtown and I want to find out more.

I've made so many trips to California and written so many stories that I've lost count. Living in Vancouver, British Columbia, I've flown to the "City of Angels" itself dozens of times. The California Tourism Board loves me. I've explored all the U.S. West Coast from Oregon down to Mexico, California inland to Palm Springs, the Temecula Valley, the Sierras, Highway 395 east of the Sierras. I've published so many travel articles in Canadian newspapers about California I should be a tour guide. When I lived in northern California for many years I drove down to San Francisco twice a week to play hockey and have a look around; over seven years I figure I've been to San Francisco at least 700 times and I never got bored. It's the world's most interesting city. But L.A. never interested me that much. Too much sprawl, smog and freeways. But things have changed.

I wander from the Marriott up Figueroa northwards, slowly, looking around. Certainly many things seem to have changed. Lots of cars and pedestrians. The first time I came to L.A. many years ago there wasn't even a downtown worthy of the name, then they started putting up skyscrapers. In the land where the automobile is king there's even a subway now. People come down to the Staples Arena via the subway for basketball, hockey and concerts. Judging by the number of new office skyscrapers, lots of people commute to work downtown too. Who'd a thunk it?

Actually, I am not in L.A. to sightsee. I am on my way to the Marquesa Islands in the South Seas, reputed to be the most beautiful place in the world, to write articles. Writers Herman Melville, Robert Louis Stevenson, Thor Heyerdahl, French painter Paul Gauguin and Belgian musician Jacques Brel moved to these islands looking for escape from the modern world. I can't imagine anyone coming to L.A. to find peace and quiet. I'm surprised at the hustle and bustle. Staying at the Marriott I am able to do what I would never have imagined doing in the past, which is to walk around downtown on foot and see what's going on, up close and first hand. Obviously things have changed a great deal.

The Tourism Bureau folks have worked out an interesting itinerary for me. They are aware of my proposed storyline of the "new L.A." and are keen to support it. The new downtown L.A. is hip, they say, full of cool bars and restaurants, funky hotels and movie stars moving from their residences out in Malibu. Judging from my previous trips to downtown L.A, I find that hard to believe. All I saw then downtown was bums looking for a handout. My walking map indicates there is a section of old downtown still marked as Skid Row. I figure I'll head in that general direction later, then to the other downtown Districts but first there is the question of lunch. I have an appointment to meet the manager at Faith and Flower, so I turn right at 9th and head east over to South Flower Street. I'm told F&F is one of the coolest restaurants downtown, and seeing as I have no aversion to fine food I head right there.

The restaurant is a contemporary design located in the WaterMarke Tower in the South Park district. The restaurant's name pays homage to the two major renaissance periods of L.A. - the 1920s and modern day - that have fundamentally shaped downtown, with "Flower" referring to the street on which the restaurant lies today, and "Faith" for the street's previous name during the early 1920s. The lunch menu runs to the usual sandwiches, burgers and pizzas, which you can get anywhere, so I go for the wild arugula salad with touches of grapefruit and Manchego cheese, mostly because it doesn't have any kale in it. These days people are putting kale even in breakfast cereals and Chinese food. I don't eat in restaurants that feature kale. Not knowing him or his sense of humour I decide not to ask the manager how wild the arugula is.

Rather than an endless discussion about the food, and how fresh it is and where it is accessed, the manager and I have a fascinating conversation about the history of L.A., especially the old downtown core and its sudden revitalization. It hadn't occurred to me before coming to research the city center's past. I was of the vague impression that L.A. was originally an orchard of some kind. I knew there was a small river from which farmers of the day accessed their water. Then William Mulholland built an aqueduct to steal water from the Sierras and the city exploded into the megalopolis it is today.

Historically, I was told, very few people lived in the downtown region because of the lack of water. Present day Los Angeles was originally home to the Chumash and Tongva Native American tribes for thousands of years. In 1781 a group of 11 families comprising 44 Mexicans settled by the river. Felipe de Neve, Governor of Spanish California, named the settlement El Pueblo Sobre el Rio de Nuestra Señora la Reina de los Angeles del Río de Porciúncula, later wisely shortened to L.A. By 1841 the first census showed a population of 141 hardy souls jabbing sticks in the ground and growing vegetables. Then in 1892 oil was discovered. As a result the city grew very rapidly and by 1900 the population was over 100,000. In 1913 Cecil B. De-Mille bought a barn in a suburb called Hollywood for film making. A light manufacturing industry grew in the downtown districts. Craft and fashion industries such as jewelry, clothing, toys and music thrived. Art deco buildings sprang up with the Roaring Twenties. To this day you can still find lovely old buildings and street signs pointing to the Fashion District, the Flower District, the Jewelry, Toy, Wholesale, Arts and other Districts.

In the early 1920s, I learned, Los Angeles was booming due to immigration. There was a burgeoning retail market downtown. Automobiles brought so many people from the newly built suburbs that multiple parking garages were constructed to alleviate the constant traffic backups. The Pacific Electric Railway system connected downtown to nearby cities like Pasadena and Whittier, as well as more far-flung places such as San Bernardino County. The booming economy and these developments made downtown attractive for architectural innovation.

From the late 1920s until the early 1940s, Art Deco was at the height of its popularity in the city. The design style included Zigzag Moderne, characterized by classic zigzag patterns and setbacks, where buildings featured a wide base, becoming narrower as they rose in height. It also included Streamline Moderne, a subdued style that emphasized horizontal design elements and often had flat roofs and curves.

While the various light manufacturing districts in the downtown area flourished over the years, the area still marked on downtown maps as Skid

Row did not. The area in which Skid Row is located was agricultural until the railroads first entered Los Angeles in the 1870s. The railroads paralleled the Los Angeles River, and the main rail yard and station were near the current Sixth Street/Whittier Boulevard river crossing. After the arrival of the railroads, the area began to modernize with an emphasis on agriculture, which is seasonal in nature and therefore requires influxes of short-term workers, especially at planting and harvesting season. The railroads themselves added to the transient nature of downtown as train crews "laid over" between assignments. As a result, many small hotels were developed in the 1880 to 1930 era to serve this worker population.

The area's proximity to the railroad station also made it the point of first arrival for all types of migrants, including those who migrated for economic reasons from elsewhere in the United States during and after each major recession or depression. Moreover, while throughout most of its history the area's population has been predominantly single and male, the recession of the 1990's resulted in many middle class families breaking up, with both single adults on their own and single adults (mostly women) with children arriving in Skid Row and in need of shelter and other assistance.

Offshoring of light manufacturing jobs in the downtown core to China began as early as the 1970s, depleting the old Art Deco buildings of many small businesses and the recession of the 1990s only exacerbated the trend. The growth in homelessness in Skid Row and the loss of small businesses turned much of the old downtown core into an expanded Skid Row. Tourists boycotted downtown. The old Art Deco buildings fell into disrepair. Then, after the 2008 economic meltdown, things started to change. Not everyone was caught up in the global economic devastation; evidently rich Chinese businesses were doing just fine and looking to invest.

In 2012, Chinese investors put $74 million into the downtown real estate market. 2014 saw a huge jump to $2.625 billion of total investment and 2015 also saw over $1.5 billion in real estate purchases. Seven percent of all Chinese investment in all of American real estate in 2016 was centered in the L.A. area, with billions in total spending. City Century (a subsidiary of Shanghai-based development firm ShengLong Group) announced plans for a massive complex near L.A. Live to include three skyscrapers, among them a 65-story tower that would be among the tallest in the city. Massive projects like Downtown's Metropolis towers and Oceanwide Plaza which cater to the ultra-wealthy were both backed by Chinese capital, "transforming LA's skyline, revitalizing neighborhoods and inspiring additional investment," according to news reports.

It's not the new skyscrapers going up that interest me today; it's the old Art Deco buildings. Thankfully they have not been torn down. Instead they are being refurbished and turned into condos and lofts for the rich newcomers and are selling like crazy. I wander into a few real estate offices and have some serious chats. There has been an enormous increase in sales and prices, I am told. Most of the new development is skewed toward higher-end property. The mix is shifting toward larger or more luxury-style products. The question for me is: Who in the world is buying all these expensive new units?

According to reports, questions were raised whether the new buildings will just become "ghost town safe deposit boxes" for their investors. Concerns have been raised that some Chinese homebuyers plan to purchase units in these new developments merely as an overseas investment with no intention of calling them home. A survey by the National Association of Realtors actually found that just 39 percent of Chinese homebuyers planned on using their U.S. property as a residence. Only time will tell who is buying, but it's certainly not American money building all these new towers.

I wander over to Broadway, which is undergoing a massive redevelopment. Old theatres like the Palace are being renovated. Gardens and flower beds and patios are being erected along the sidewalks. The pawn shops and jewelry stores are gradually disappearing. I wander into pawn shops and a jewelry store and enjoy a conversation with an employee, a lady of Persian descent. She gives me a poster being distributed to shops throughout the District showing a streetscape master plan for the future. News reports call it a "bellwether of significant changes."

Taking up some of the most beautiful and unique historic structures in California , the Jewelry District grew rapidly in response to Downtown L.A.'s demise as buildings hollowed out in the 70s and 80s, becoming seedy and covered in layers of thick grime. The days of shutting down promptly at 5 P.M. with ghetto-style roll-down gates and turning into a scary ghost town have finally stumbling to an end. Things are afoot.

I ride the elevators to the top of the Standard, once a bank but now a hip hotel. The top floor has a bar with a live band playing, a swimming pool and some of the hippest dudes and babes in all of L.A. laying back and soaking up the sun. I wander the streets of the Arts District as well, with artists at hand sketching landscapes with hundreds of their paintings set out for display and sale. At night I take the suggestion from the concierge at my hotel to ride a cab down to Bestia, at the moment the hottest restaurant in town but located in a portion of Skid Row where I am informed it is not advisable to wander at night. Street people are numerous.

According to its website, "the concept for Bestia juxtaposes decorative contemporary elements against a raw, industrial space dripping with character. This approach pays homage to sophisticated modern-day Italian spaces, which often integrate contemporary interiors into centuries-old structures. Strong, traditional building materials such as tile, steel, marble, and wood also provide pops of festive color. The name Bestia (Italian for 'Beast') echoes throughout the space via hard-edged design elements, such as the wall covering's pattern of bar-fight weapons, intimidating meat-hook chandeliers suspended from soaring steel tracks, and bathroom tile work that reads as unfinished." Whatever.

There is a line to get in. The place is packed. I can barely hear myself think. Despite the prior pleadings of the Tourism Bureau folks on my behalf I can't secure a table, but a single seat has been made available for an important guy like me at the bar. This is fine with me as my elevated position allows me to have a good look around. The phrase "beautiful people" comes to mind. Nobody is dressed up, but they sure look attractive. L.A. is like that. On an earlier trip I had strolled down Rodeo Boulevard in Beverly Hills with the vague idea that I would sneak inside the finest boutiques in the world and take some surreptitious photos of the beautiful people shopping there, an idea for a story. The gigantic doormen standing guard in their thousand dollar suits and watching carefully made sure that story didn't happen, but I noticed that much of the sales staff on Rodeo was even better looking than the customers. Now the beautiful people are also shopping downtown.

Sitting next to my right at the Bestia's bar is someone I feel I have seen before. I hesitate to ask him if we know each other, because at six feet four and maybe 240 pounds he is even bigger than I am, and very muscular, but I feel I know him. The gentleman in question is sitting next to a lady I would rate as an eleven on a beauty scale of one to ten. Her smile alone would blow the lights out, a dazzling array of pearly whites, but it is her date's teeth that finally solve the puzzle. I realize he is a hockey player with the L.A. Kings and I have seen him on TV many times. He is missing a front tooth. You would think with the money that professional athletes make he could afford to fix his teeth, but maybe they just get knocked out in the next fist fight. The menu is all in Italian so I settle for a pizza and hail a cab for the ride back to the Marriott because even at my size I am not going to walk through Skid Row in the dark.

According to Jones Lang LaSalle, a major L.A. commercial leasing company, Los Angeles ranks number two in North America, just behind New York and ahead of San Francisco, and number eight globally, as one of the key cities involved in China's future investment plans. Chinese companies invested 38 billion U.S. dollars into firms in the United States in 2020, when measured on a historical-cost basis. According to Public Citizen, Chinese financial interests have acquired more than $120 billion of assets in the U.S. economy since 2002. Fifteen Chinese government entities (sovereign wealth funds and state-owned enterprises) and government-connected private sectors firms account for nearly 60 percent of this activity. Major transactions have been recorded in at least 40 U.S. states and in diverse sectors.

I have a plane to catch later in the evening to Tahiti, so I stroll back to the Marriott amazed at the hustle and bustle downtown, people thronging the streets and the line-ups at the bars and restaurants. There is money everywhere, and I begin to wonder where it is all coming from. Until now I thought it was just Vancouver that was being overwhelmed by Chinese investment. It suddenly appears that the phenomenon is more widespread than I had realized.

PING-PONG DIPLOMACY

Just like with Covid 19, it is necessary to trace any disease back to its beginning in order to find ways to overcome it. In the case of the pandemic, many scientists say it was wet markets in China selling animal meats, markets which still exist in abundance and the CCP government has made no effort to close them down. Aside from the elites, the majority

31

of people in China remain poor and don't shop in fancy supermarkets. It should be remembered that Ebola started in Africa with poor people eating game, and the swine flu started in Mexico from a lack of sanitation. As long as people continue to eat meat we will have outbreaks.

As for the "American disease," (i.e. "the end justifies the means," even if it's illegal) you need to go far back to ascertain when this incestuous relationship with the CCP commenced. Hard to believe but it all started in 1971 with a ping pong game, which soon led to the phrase "ping-pong diplomacy." This refers to the exchange of table tennis players between the United States and People's Republic of China during the 1971 World Table Tennis Championships in Nagoya, Japan. At this time the United States viewed the People's Republic of China (PRC) as an aggressor nation and enforced an economic containment policy including an embargo on the PRC, following the PRC's entry into the Korean War in 1950. But somehow the relationship slowly changed, or you might say some politicians on both sides wanted a change in relations, each for their own economic purpose.

In July 1971, President Nixon's National Security Advisor Henry Kissinger had secretly visited Beijing during a trip to Pakistan, and laid the groundwork for Nixon's future visit to China. This meeting was arranged and facilitated by Pakistan through its strong diplomatic channels with China. Until that time, China and the U.S. were direct enemies, with the U.S. fighting a war in Vietnam to stop the spread of communism and maintaining troops in Korea.

Then ranked 23rd in the world, the U.S. ping pong team was comprised of amateur players paying their own expenses to travel to the World

Table Tennis Championships in Nagoya, Japan where they first met their Chinese counterparts. The Chinese team's superiority was clear: across the seven events at the Championships, they won four gold, three silver and two bronze medals. The Americans left empty-handed. Following the championships, the U.S. team was invited to China for a short tour, where they had a chance to visit the Great Wall. On Premier Zhou Enlai's orders, the Chinese prioritized "friendship first, competition second," deliberately losing some of the games. The tour, quickly dubbed "ping-pong diplomacy" by the American press, was historic for its political rather than its sporting consequences.

Less than a year later, U.S. basketball players, various physicists and the Philadelphia Orchestra visited. China subsequently sent an array of sporting and cultural delegations to the US. "Ping-pong diplomacy" is also sometimes referred to as the first time a group of Americans had ever visited the PRC but this claim is not quite true. Over 40 of the 160 young Americans who travelled to the Sixth World Festival of Youth and Students, held in Moscow in 1957, continued on to China, where Zhou Enlai welcomed them as "pioneers in opening the contacts between the people of the two countries."

That visit received worldwide press attention, not least because the young Americans, many of them teenagers, were knowingly violating a US government ban on all travel to the PRC imposed in 1952. But their trip had little effect on diplomatic relation because the US State Department made good on its promise to seize the passports of the attendees and threatened to imprison any other Americans bold enough to follow in their footsteps. Amazing how times changed when the American media found out there was going to be free Chinese food on the upcoming press trip.

By 1971 the situation concerning communism had changed. Nixon, who had been Eisenhower's vice president, made it clear in a 1967 Foreign Affairs article that he no longer supported a policy of isolating China. Some contact with a country of a billion people had to be restored, he argued. Like Eisenhower, however, Nixon worried about a public backlash against any effort to negotiate with Beijing. When he and Kissinger opened a highly secretive backchannel to Mao and Zhou in 1970, they avoided using the White House letterhead for fear that Beijing would leak their correspondence. Yes, it's hard to justify a trip to "meet with the enemy" after 50,000 young American men came home in body bags from Vietnam, never mind what transpired in Korea.

One important moment at the Ping Pong Championships did, however, occur only by chance. American and Chinese players and officials had already conversed on the sidelines of the games in Japan. Graham Steenhoven, the president of the US Table Tennis Association, pointedly told his Chinese counterpart, Song Zhong, that Nixon had recently rescinded the ban on travel to the PRC violated by the 1957 youth delegation. But the real breakthrough occurred when the U.S. player Glenn Cowan accidentally boarded the Chinese team's bus. An awkward silence was broken by the Chinese team captain Zhuang Zedong. As they got off the bus, Zhuang presented Cowan with a silk-screen depiction of China's Huangshan Mountains to rapid-fire clicks from gathered U.S. press cameras. Perhaps Zhuang had brought the gift to Japan to give to an American. Perhaps it was just one of the tokens the Chinese carried for friendly interactions with rival teams. In any case, the ping pong interactions caused a severe reaction. Hey, never mind communism; American and China were suddenly buddies, and what could be better than that? No doubt Henry Kissinger was as pleased as could be.

CHAPTER FOUR

THE SOUTH SEAS

We have always known that heedless self-interest was bad morals, we now know that it is bad economics.
                                                    – Franklin Delano Roosevelt

Tahiti! Tah-HEET-ee! Just the blend of sharp consonants spoken together with the tongue clicking against your teeth evokes dreams of an earthly paradise. Imagined from a distance, the Polynesian islands are a lush tropical playground to which those in a madding modern western world full of worry and tension aspire to visit, at least for a romantic holiday. Since its discovery a few centuries ago, Westerners have travelled to the South Seas as an escape and sometimes in an attempt to change their lives. Famous writers and artists like Herman Melville, Robert Louis Stevenson, Jack London, Thor Heyerdahl, Belgian singer Jacques Brel and French artist Paul Gauguin have ventured or moved to the South Seas and written about their adventures. They painted images of an exotic dreamland that, sadly, never really existed or only existed to some small degree before the arrival of the invading colonial powers.

After a very long flight from L.A. I arrive too late at Faa'a International Airport outside Papeete, the capital city of Tahiti (and of the Polynesian territories) to meet my Polynesian Tourism Board guide. The plane was late leaving Los Angeles, where an overzealous teenage security guard making minimum wage seized both my water bottle and toothpaste. There was a dribble of water in the bottle after I had poured it out in the washroom, and my toothpaste tube, half full, was deemed to be a serious security threat. This sort of uptight anal retentive behavior stands in sharp contrast to my arrival at F'aaa airport, where my guide has gotten bored waiting for me to arrive and simply left, leaving me to find my own way to town and the ferry dock.

At the ferry, I revert to my very rusty high school French. Evidently for some reason my guide has already gone ahead to Moorea, Tahiti's sister island and our planned destination for today, and the ferry staff say I should meet her there even though I don't have a ticket to get there, because she has it. Whatever. I manage to explain and am let aboard.

Everything in French Polynesia is French, including the language and customs. Few people speak a word of English, including the Polynesians. It soon becomes clear that Polynesia is a French colony, with all that word implies. Time is a theoretical concept; no one worries about issues like punctuality. The Polynesians are extremely relaxed while the French prove, as I have learned elsewhere in my global travels, rude and conde-scending. The so-called "work ethic" here is non-existent. The capital city of Papeete, surprisingly, is a dump and everything is imported and very expensive. Moorea, a short ferry ride away, is simply a suburb of Papeete, along with a couple of beach resorts. Few tourists stay on the island of Ta-hiti; they land at the F'aaa airport and transfer to flights to Bora Bora and other more visually appealing destinations.

But as time goes by it becomes obvious that the outside world, a million miles away, doesn't exist here to any great degree. This discovery is utterly delightful. Of all the remote places on the planet I have visited, Polynesia is one of the few where the ongoing and endless crises of America and Europe don't exist. It is the modern world, not Polynesia, which is actually off the map here. It is indeed a delight to arrive in a place where the modern world is so far away that its crises do not require my strict attention.

My assignment in the South Seas is certainly not a hardship adventure. I am to live aboard the *Aranui 3* for a few weeks, a cargo ship that accepts up to 200 passengers on its way through various assorted atolls to deliv-er freight to the Marquesa Islands, which, according to the Polynesian Tourism Board, is "the most remote destination in the world" because that island group is the farthest away from any large land mass such as a continent. The *Aranui 3* delivers everything from cars to satellite dishes to junk food to the Marquesan islands, which survive mainly as an exotic tourist destination for rich French bourgeoisie to visit when they are fed up with life in Paris.

It is within only a day or so aboard the ship that I sadly notice im-ported European diseases such as cultural tension and racism have been imported on the *Aranui*. In short, the French bourgeoisie treat the other passengers with contempt and the Germans and English don't like such rudeness, or each other, or the French either. Given that Polynesia is a French colony, the Parisian bourgeoisie act as if it is their right to jump queues and skip past line-ups, both at meal times and while boarding whaleboats to go ashore. Fifty percent of the passengers are French, I learn, although not all are rich, so some actually behave themselves. Perhaps a third is German. I am informed by a Canadian passenger who has ventured forth to the Marquesas several times in her search for paradise that by the end of the voyage the Germans may be throwing the French bourgeoisie overboard for their snotty behavior. The British passengers queue automatically, because they have good manners but they mutter about those that don't wait in line, and of course the Brits don't like the Germans. The Americans don't notice anything amiss because they are totally self-absorbed, as a good American always will be, and they don't speak any foreign languages.

Otherwise, aside from these imported First World tensions, the Marquesan and Tahitian crews blissfully go about their duties, silent and stoic. While the French are in control of the bureaucracy, this is still a Polynesian culture. Interestingly, the mammoth economic and military power of the United States is virtually invisible in Polynesia. The French here still consider themselves to be a global super power; no mention of America is found in the local media. The emerging Cold War between America and China might as well be taking place on Mars. Russia does not exist here either. Climate change, however, is a harsh reality for those South Sea Islands that soon may be under water, but no one seems to want to discuss such negative matters. This is Polynesia. This is paradise.

On the way to the Marquesas I schedule a meeting with the owner of the ship, Mr. Wong. The *Aranui 3* is a unique vessel. La Compagnie Polynesienne de Transport Maritime, also known as C.P.T.M, is a third-generation Chinese maritime company which operates the *Aranui*. Founded in 1954 by the patriarch of the Wong family of Tahiti, first as Wing Man Hing and subsequently as C.P.T.M., their ships have been plying the waters of French Polynesia for over six decades. Originally, the company also serviced the Tuamotu and Gambier Archipelagos, supplying and conducting trade between these islands and Tahiti.

In 1978, as Mr. Wong reports to me when we meet, the commercial line to the Marquesas Islands was added to C.P.T.M's shipping route, and in 1984, the *Aranui 3* was converted to accommodate passengers, creating Aranui Cruises. At the time of its first sailing and for many years after, the Aranui was the only ship to take tourists to the Marquesas, putting these far-flung islands finally on the map and creating global interest in this little-known archipelago.

Should you stick your nose into the economic history of the South Seas, you will find that outside colonial powers from France to Great Britain have also stuck their own noses into paradise. British Captain Bligh, sad figure behind the "Mutiny on the *Bounty*" fiasco, was assigned to grow breadfruit on Tahiti to transport to the Caribbean to feed slaves on the British plantations there. The French arrived not far behind the British and still maintain Polynesia as an overseas domain. Somehow in all this outside interference by great powers we are forgetting the Chinese. As the old joke goes, everywhere you go in the world you will find a Chinese grocery store. In the South Seas, the Chinese remain quietly in the background, but like many other regions of the world today they are starting to take control.

According to the *Asia Times*, the Chinese government (I.E. the CCP or the Chinese Communist Party) has an official plan for its conquest of the South Pacific. For starters, the CCP's militarization of islands in the South China Sea is by now viewed by the U.S. as a threat to freedom of navigation in one of the world's most strategically important waterways. Awareness is now emerging that the CCP wants to use those emerging forward bases to project power all over the Pacific, where political analysts claim the CCP harbors "neo-colonial" ambitions of its own, and where the United States maintains a crucial naval and air force base on Guam.

A Pentagon report states China's training for air strikes against the U.S. and allied targets will soon bring the CCP's emerging power projection capabilities in the Pacific into stark and urgent relief among policymakers in Washington. The report indicates these training flights are also designed to influence island nations in the South Pacific, where China's rapid advance southward is already viewed with concern by the U.S.

With a strong foothold in the South China Sea now, China can project military power across the Pacific Islands at a time when its fishing fleets are also increasing their presence there. Bases in the South China Sea's Spratly and Paracel island chains, from which Peoples Liberation Army strategic bombers can reach well into the South Seas, now back Beijing's economic and political ambitions in various Pacific Islands. Naval and aviation support facilities on Fiery Cross, Subi, and Mischief Reefs are roughly 1,500 miles closer to Oceania than mainland China bases. Ongoing construction on these three major outposts increases Beijing's ability to impose force in the poorly defended region.

U.S. Navy intelligence officers claim that China's militarization of South China Sea islands plays into its larger scheme of regional hegemony, paving the way for port leases and maritime construction efforts while making a powerful play for this resource-rich, strategically crucial region, all the way from the continent of Australia to other less-populated

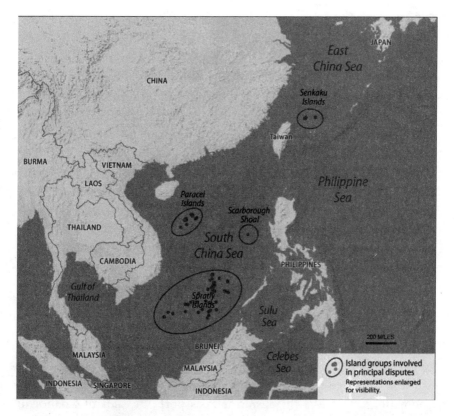

island nations. China's claim to most of the 3.5 million square kilometer South China Sea was ruled illegal by a Permanent Arbitral Tribunal at The Hague, a ruling the CCP has simply ignored. China started to militarize the South China Sea in 2015, despite a promise by Chinese President Xi Jinping not to do so. PLA Air long-range, nuclear strike-capable H-6K bombers can attack targets as much as 3,300 kilometers away, or deep into the Pacific Islands and down to Australia. It is also a key step in China advancing its status as a Pacific Ocean power intent on rivaling America's long-standing predominance in the area.

According to a US-China Economic and Security Review Commission, Beijing has significantly bolstered its economic ties within Oceania. China has growing geo-strategic interests in the region. It is the largest trading partner with Pacific Island countries, with annual trade totaling over $8.2 billion U.S. China is deeply involved with Pacific Island regional organizations, for which it often provides funding and other support. Beijing's strategy for achieving its aims in the Pacific starts with financial aid, political donations and investments that pave commercial inroads and an increase in Chinese migration to the region.

Australia's Lowy Institute think-tank reports China's financial aid commitment to the Pacific Islands has skyrocketed to $5.9 billion U.S., about two-thirds disbursed as loans, with only a third given as grants. China's interest-bearing loans have saddled many countries worldwide with unsustainable "debt traps." This debt allows Beijing to take control of the cash-strapped debtor nations' ports and other facilities as partial repayment.

China has started using "weaponized tourism" to force some small island nations to submit to Beijing's foreign policy directions. The CCP effectively banned tour groups and further investment in Palua, an idyllic tropic archipelago. Its empty hotel rooms, idle tour boats, and shuttered construction sites are the result of economic warfare against Palau for its continued diplomatic relations with Taiwan. There are also sound economic reasons for China to be in the South Pacific, including sourcing raw materials. Many of the South Pacific islands are rich with resources such as timber, minerals and fish. Since 2011, the CCP has invested heavily in Papua New Guinea, which is home to gold and nickel mines, liquefied natural gas and timber forests.

Another rising concern for Pacific Islanders is fast-shifting demographics. Island nations have small Indigenous populations that could easily be swamped by Chinese immigration, especially now that many island nations are selling citizenship and passports. In Vanuatu, a nation of less than 300,000 people, there are plans to build two Chinese cities that could each host a total of 10,000 to 20,000 Chinese immigrants. Island nation leaders are concerned about losing control of their economies to the influx of Chinese workers and wealthy Chinese expats who live in walled compounds. Some Pacific Islanders have used the term "colonialism" to describe largely unchecked Chinese investment and immigration. Fear is that in the next 10 years, some islands will be controlled by the Chinese.

Statistics on the number of Chinese living in the South Pacific are scarce, but back in 2006 the South Pacific islands were already home to an estimated 80,000 Chinese. Some were descended from Chinese traders who settled in the region in the 1800s, while others migrated more recently to work on Chinese construction projects. China has built a new wharf on the Vanuatu island of Espiritu Santo, making it one of the largest ports in the South Pacific. It has built sports stadiums, convention centers, roads, airport upgrades, office buildings for Vanuatu's Foreign Affairs, and the Prime Minister's new office.

Chinese interest in French Polynesia also stems from access to the rich fishery resources of the so-called "tuna belt" as well as its use in space exploration activities. The islands also provide a refueling and transshipment point between China and the Americas that could support PLA operations in the future. China has invested $330 million U.S. for an aquaculture project in French Polynesia's large and remote Hao atoll, an investment that surpasses all foreign direct investment received by French Polynesia for several years. The atoll once supported France's nuclear testing program and is home to an airport that has the capacity to support strategic bombers.

French Polynesia is already home to a large Chinese community, with five to ten percent of its total population being of Chinese origin. The first Chinese migrants arrived in Tahiti in the 1860s, mostly as plantation workers, and Chinese immigrants to Tahiti have contributed largely to the territory's economy. Robert Wan, the son of a Chinese immigrant, introduced oyster farms to French Polynesia in the 1970s. China is one of French Polynesia's main trade partners; 10 percent of Tahitian imports come from China, and a third of Tahitian exports go to Hong Kong, mostly in the form of pearls. Tourism has been a major economic sector for French Polynesia, comprising more than 12 percent of its GDP.

China's strategic and military interests in the South Pacific are expanding rapidly. In an article in *The Diplomat*, it is explained they are filling the vacuum left by receding U.S. and French influence, as well as Australia and New Zealand's longstanding neglect of close relationships. China has offered what the United States and its allies cannot, massive sums of money for development projects that promise jobs and economic independence.

But Pacific Ocean nations are gradually learning the true cost. Take, for instance, the scandal over the Chinese consulate in Tahiti's illegal occupation of a house used for China's diplomatic offices in French Polynesia. Built in an imposing French colonial style on a prominent site, the Chinese consulate has been renting the property since 2007. The property owners say that China never respected the terms of the rental agreement, so in 2017 they refused to renew the lease. According to the rental agreement, the building was to be used for accommodation purposes only but China turned the house into diplomatic offices and did not pay rubbish collection fees for 10 years. They denied the property owner the right to inspect the property regularly and installed a satellite dish on the roof of the house without permission. The consulate was told to evacuate the property but the consul refused to leave and demanded the owner sell the house to China. Consular staff claimed in a letter that "once rented, the house has become territory of the People's Republic of China."

Satellite interests are an important aspect of China's surge into the South Pacific. The PLA recently launched 18 BeiDou-3 satellites into space that will provide missile positioning and timing and enhanced C4ISR (Command, Control, Communications, Computers, Intelligence, Surveillance and Reconnaissance) capabilities for the Chinese military, as well as navigation services to more than 60 countries along its expanding Belt and Road initiative, including those in Oceania. Papeete is where China's mobile satellite-receiving vessel as well as other military boats regularly dock.

During my discussion with Mr. Wong I discover that the shipping business is so good that the *Aranui 3* will soon be replaced by a larger vessel, the *Aranui 5*. As a writer I have difficulty with mathematics and need to take off my socks to count to ten, but it is clear even to a moron such as me that the number four has been skipped. I inquire as to its disappearance. Mr. Wong looks at me as if I am stupid, which apparently I am. The number four, he says with grim seriousness, is very unlucky. The number is not spoken of in Chinese, and rarely seen. Think of it as the Chinese version of thirteen, deemed to be an unlucky number by some in the western world, only the number four in Chinese is far more serious.

Apparently number four in Chinese has a pronunciation that is similar to the word for death. I had some previous vague knowledge of this and decided to do some research. While the number four is unlucky, the number eight is the opposite, which is very lucky. As well as eight, Chinese superstitions say that the numbers 88, 18 and 168 are also lucky, so they are well sought after in the housing market. Some builders skip any floors with the number four involved, such as 14, 24, 34 and all 40 to 49 floors. Chinese people enjoy superstitions so much that they've even adopted the Western superstition of the unlucky number thirteen. Six is also considered lucky because it is a homonym for the word "flow" or "smooth" (liu). Therefore, the number six is often used when starting a new business. On the other hand, seven is considered unlucky because it coincides with the seventh lunar month of the Chinese calendar, the "ghost month," when it is said the gates of hell open and ghosts wander the human world in search of food.

My own grandmother subscribed to a special set of her own superstitions, but I understand that she was bereft of any kind of formal education and reverted to superstition to fill the void. Superstition often fills the bill for those who have limited education, but I considered the Chinese to be well educated, or educated enough not to believe in such nonsense, but my research revealed this is not the case at all. I am shocked to learn how deeply superstition permeates Chinese culture all around the world. Those doing business with the Chinese need to pay attention.

Take the instance of the Beijing Olympics and its grand opening ceremony. It's no coincidence that the games commenced at 8:08 PM on August 8th, 2008. If someone starts a new business in China, some Chinese business people will turn to a fortune teller for guidance and pay a considerable amount of money to learn the exact time to open their business. When a person's Zodiac animal will occur the next year, this means that it will be a tough year for them so they should purchase red socks or underwear to protect themselves.

When you think about it, you don't often see a Chinese man with a beard. That is because the Chinese believe that one should keep a well-shaven face. At the very least, a moustache should be well-trimmed. It's another Chinese superstition as they believe any facial hair that looks shabby is considered bad luck. Even when it comes to designing the family home, the Chinese are superstitious. They believe that the building should not face the north as it would bring bad fortune to the family.

The color white is known as one of the unluckiest Chinese colors because it is associated with mourning and loss. You will often see Chinese people wearing white to funerals. The color green is considered to be unlucky as it is associated with infidelity. A man wearing a green hat is said to have an unfaithful wife. The color black is considered to be unlucky as well given its association to the darkness and secrecy. The word "mafia" translates to "black society" in Chinese. On the other hand, it doesn't get much better than the color red in China. It's the color of the flag, and it represents happiness. During weddings or festivals, you'll see red everywhere. In particular, during the Spring Festival, children will be given a red envelope full of money as a good luck present.

The poor old turtle isn't well regarded in Chinese superstition. If a turtle is kept as a pet it will ruin the home owner's business and fortune because a turtle will slow down the person's business. Chinese superstition doesn't stop there. Chinese noodles are long because uncut noodles in soup will increase longevity. If the noodles are cut it will "cut the longevity." If you get too full to finish your bowl of rice, don't stick your chopsticks in there because it resembles the sight of incense at a tomb.

It is believed that pregnant women should never attend funerals or weddings, avoid getting a stroller before the baby is born, and not visit houses that have been vacant for a long time because they are considered spiritually unclean, which means dangerous entities may be present. In

Chinese culture, people will burn fake paper money to commemorate a person who has passed away. Do not use a broom to clean the floor on the first day of Chinese New Year. Do not throw out the trash on this day, or clean your house, especially the floors, because the broom is seen as making fortune go away.

Don't give gifts that bring bad luck like an umbrella, clocks, or knives. The words sound very similar to things with darker meanings. Clock (sòng zhōng) sounds like "attending a funeral." Knives, scissors, nail clippers or anything sharp signifies the cutting of bonds or severing of friendships. Umbrella (san) sounds exactly like the word for "breaking up." Pears are never given as a gift because pears (lí) sounds just like the term for "to part."

My tour of the Marquesas is as eye-opening as was my later research into Chinese superstitions. While the landscape is beautiful the history is not. Guided tours of ancient sites reveal a sobering past. The people were fierce warriors, headhunters and cannibals. They sometimes ate their enemies, referring to them as "long pig." Islanders fought other islanders to the death. Skulls were stacked high on stages in the villages. When Europeans arrived they brought hideous diseases that almost wiped out the native population. The Roman Catholic Church went on a campaign to wipe out any traces of the former pagan culture. It is only recently that the Marquesan people are regaining the use of their own language. There are, strangely enough, no Chinese grocery stores or Chinese restaurants on any of the islands. The open air restaurant Yvonne's on the north side of Niku Hiva serves up an excellent roast pig, but you need rather a large crowd like from the *Aranui 3* to order and eat one, while the roast goat is said to be good as well.

CHAPTER FIVE

THE LAND OF OZ

Our economy is based on spending billions to persuade people that happiness is buying things, and then insisting that the only way to have a viable economy is to make things for people to buy so they'll have jobs and get enough money to buy things.

                                                        – Philip Slater

For some reason I've always liked Australians. There are a lot of Aussies where I live in Canada, drawn by the opportunity to go skiing while on a two-year work visa, which is allowed because both countries are part of the British Commonwealth. Aussies strike me as a cheerful people, always ready with a "no worries, mate" when faced with any problem. So when the Queensland Tourism Bureau offers me an invitation to come to the Great Barrier Reef to learn how to scuba dive – and publish a story about it, of course – I accept with full grace and humility. It's a long way from Canada to Down Under, and I may have mentioned that long ago I had learned the First Law of Journalism (which is "never pay for your own drinks") can be adapted to "never pay for your own global travels if you can find a way to get them for free."

As explained earlier I had already come to the sad realization that Vancouver, while a beautiful place when it is not raining, is the most over-priced city in the world if you consider the average annual income compared to the ever-rising and sky-high cost of living. So it was with great surprise that I discover that the basic necessities of life, like pizza and beer, cost even more in Sydney than back home! Actually, Sydney is located nowhere near the Great Barrier Reef but international flights land in Sydney and I want to visit my friend "Also Named Michael," who I had met while we were both in Cambodia enjoying adventures, like the time our overloaded ferry boat almost sank in the great inland sea called the Tonle Sap, which was conveniently full of crocodiles looking for tourists to gnosh on. We kindly requested that the captain jump overboard and find the hole in the hull, which turned out he had made when he smashed into the dock near Angkor Wat, and Also Named Michael and I had been friends ever since.

Michael and his wife and son live in a small flat some distance from downtown Sydney, as close to downtown as they could afford under the circumstances. He works in the world of finance, a job where he was paid good money. His wife also had a good job, but real estate prices in Sydney were so high that they couldn't afford to live any closer to downtown. This comes as a surprise to me. Australia is on the other side of the word from Canada and news of Oz is hard to come by, so I had no idea what the Chinese financial invasion of Australia had done to the cost of living there. While Vancouver is the first stepping stone into North America for Chinese money and immigrants, Australia is a lot closer to China and hot Chinese money had been arriving in Sydney for several years and has made a huge impact.

To celebrate my arrival we all go out for dinner and Michael is paying. We split a pizza four ways and have a beer, and the damage comes to what it would cost a person in Des Moines to buy a used car. Their little flat in an ordinary neighborhood is worth a million Canadian dollars. He can't afford to own a car. Thanks to Chinese investment, the cost of everything has skyrocketed. In most countries he would be considered rich but in Sydney Michael is fighting to keep above the survival line. I am "gob smacked," as the English would say. Who knew? First Los Angeles, then Sydney. Chinese money was infiltrating everywhere.

As can be expected, just like the 19th century Gold Rush in British Columbia and the one in California in 1849, the number of Chinese people in Australia rose significantly during the Aussie gold rush era, and by 1861 was around 40,000 immigrants, constituting about three percent of the total population. Australia has been a haven for Chinese migrants ever since who have established themselves as a significant minority group. There are now large populations of Australian-born Chinese and Chinese-born migrants in the cities of Melbourne, Sydney, and Brisbane with small Chinese communities in regional centers, particularly in Victoria and New South Wales. There are also Chinatowns in every Australian capital city, including Darwin in the north, and large public Chinese New Year Celebrations in Melbourne and Sydney.

The current, close history between the two countries goes back quite a while. After the establishment of the People's Republic of China (PRC) in 1949 and the subsequent retreat of the Republic of China (ROC) government to Taiwan, Australia refused to recognize the communist PRC.

During the Cold War, Australia's strategic alignment swung towards the United States. While the Labour Party's official policy from 1955 was that Australia should follow the examples of Britain and France in recognizing the PRC, on the basis that the ROC was unlikely to recover the mainland, the Liberal Party played up the perceived threat of a Communist China for an electoral advantage. As part of this political strategy, Prime Minister Harold Holt explicitly recognized the continuing legitimacy of the ROC government in Taiwan in 1966 by sending an ambassador to Taipei for the first time. However, as an opposition leader, Gough Whitlam visited mainland China in 1971 (before Henry Kissinger's historic secret visit on behalf of the United States), and in December 1972, after victory in that year's federal election, Australia finally established diplomatic relations with the PRC, and Australia ceased to recognize the Republic of China government of Chiang Kai-shek in Taiwan.

Since the Chinese economic reforms, usually understood as being initiated by Deng Xiaoping in the late 1970s, the CCP has benefited from significant investment in mainland China by Australian companies while Australia has also benefited from the Chinese appetite for natural resources to modernize its economy, infrastructure and to meet its growing energy demands. By 2009, it was estimated the trade and investment with China brought benefits of close to $4,000 per Australian household; in 2011, it was estimated to be $10,500 per household per year. Massive, mate! Australia was one of the few countries in the world during the global financial crisis of 2008 that did not go into recession. Its continued economic growth during that period is partly attributed to large demand and long-term strong investment from China.

As China's influence in Australia has increased, the Chinese government in Beijing has been trying to control and monitor the ethnic Chinese living and studying in Australia and to influence Australian politicians via political donations, which has caused serious concern to Australia's security agency. Meanwhile, with the rise of Xi Jinping as the CCP's Commander in Chief and his threats towards his country's own ethnic minorities and to neighboring countries, a group of 39 countries, including Australia, made a statement in 2020 at the United Nations to denounce China for its treatment of ethnic minorities and for curtailing freedoms in Hong Kong.

Immediately China's embassy released a list of Chinese grievances against Australia. The list includes such issues as government funding for "anti-China" research at the Australian Strategic Policy Institute, raids on

Chinese journalists and academic visa cancellations, "spearheading a crusade" in multilateral forums on China's affairs in Taiwan, Hong Kong and Xinjiang, and for Australia calling for an independent investigation into the origins of COVID-19. A Chinese embassy official stated: "China is angry. If you make China the enemy, China will be the enemy." The official said that if Australia backed away from the policies on the list, it would be "conducive to a better atmosphere." The statement was seen as an open threat by the CCP towards Australia.

In 2021, Australia announced a complex plan to purchase American nuclear submarines, in cooperation with Great Britain, a key element of the new AUKUS political-military alignment. Although China was not specifically mentioned in the news announcements, critics interpreted it as a major blow to the Australian-Chinese relationship by firmly allying Australia with the United States in military terms in the South Pacific region. Soon after, Chinese military ships were seen cruising near Australia at a time when Australian defense force exercises were also taking place. Australian Defense minister Peter Dutton said that he was shocked to see Chinese ships maneuvering so close to his country.

Also Named Michael's father has a power boat so I received a personal tour by Michael of world famous Sydney Harbor. We picnicked on a sandbar right across from the world famous Opera House. After that, we motor up the harbour under the gigantic Sydney Bridge and north to Darlington to visit one of the biggest seafood markets I have ever seen. Sydney, like Vancouver and other West Coast cities in North America, is very modern and has grown immensely, with a downtown core of sparkling glass towers.

Cairns proves a big surprise as well. Until such time as I was invited to come to Queensland I had never heard of Cairns. It was officially founded in 1876 as a frontier town to support the gold rush. The city took its name from the State Governor of the day, Sir William Cairns. The initial site for Cairns was a sandy bank lined with dense rainforest and mangroves. The swamps are still there but there is a port at the mouth of the river where cruise ships tie up. Today the population is 155,000, and maybe closer to 200,000 if you count all the Chinese tourists swarming the streets on my arrival.

Cairns enjoys a modern airport on which planes touch down from Sydney and other distant points. The town is one of the scuba diving capitals of the world, thanks to the Great Barrier Reef that lies hidden under water about 100 miles offshore. The Tourism Board wants me to join half a dozen other travel writers from around the world and learn how to scuba dive, and then publish an article on the topic in Canadian newspapers. I have carefully refrained from taking any relevant medical tests in Canada, mostly because the tests cost a lot of money and aren't covered by medicare. "No worries, mate," came the reply from the Tourism Board when I updated them on my status, "there's a clinic on every corner in Cairns and the tests only cost five dollars."

Given that I play competitive hockey several times a week and sprint over a hundred miles a week on my bike I was not worried about any physical exams. However, "no worries" turns to real worry when I fail my breathing test at the clinic in Cairns. I need to blow into a balloon, which is easy, but I need to reach 90 on the dial and I only hit 82. Something to do with aging; when you pass a certain number your lung capacity decreases. Sorry, no medical certificate for scuba diving today.

The Tourism Board is not fazed with the result in the slightest. No worries, mate. Instead of spending four days in a motel swimming pool to learn the scuba equipment, I can tour the Daintree Rainforest instead and then snorkel the Great Barrier Reef with the other divers, and thereby write several stories. I had no idea there was a rainforest in Australia. Evidently it's been there over 40,000 years so I should have heard a few rumors by now, but no. The excursions through the Daintree Rainforest and mountains and nearby Mariba wetlands prove far more interesting than spending four dang days dog paddling in a swimming pool, and I have several wonderful adventures except for all the people driving on the wrong side of the road, which may be why Oz is called Down Under.

I do more research. According to Politico, not that long ago Australia thought it was building a nice friendship with China. The federal government wanted to teach Mandarin in schools and invited the Chinese president to address parliament. Happy days. Now, that BS is done with. Australia is buying nuclear-powered submarines, barring China from key markets and seething at the CCP's relentless attempts to coerce Australian politicians and media. The anger of the Aussies reflects rising global wariness of China's increasingly threatening behavior.

Chinese Premier Xi Jinping is increasing his relentless attempts to control the economic and cultural climate overseas, but obviously some of his bullying tactics have rapidly boomeranged. Instead of forcing Australia into submission, Xi's "wolf warrior" tactics have turned Australia right back to its traditional military partners the United States and United Kingdom. The phrase "wolf-warrior" is named after a popular Chinese action film, denoting that China is no longer content to exercise its former "soft power" policy of quietly infiltrating other country's economies, using the fortunes they have made through unbalanced trade deals with wealthy western business executives thirsting after new markets and profits.

When Xi took control of the Chinese Communist Party in 2012, the Australian government was in the midst of a geo-strategic pivot. During that year Australia wrote the Asian Century White Paper, setting out national objectives that included moving away from its colonial Commonwealth roots and position as America's deputy sheriff in the Asia-Pacific, and towards carving out a role as a regional power in its own right. Canberra turned to Beijing, its top trading partner, for a landmark free-trade agreement. Xi was even invited to address a joint sitting of Australia's parliament, an honor usually reserved for U.S. commanders-in-chief.

While Australia was moving towards a partnership with China, Beijing was telling a different story to its own people. Xi had delivered a very different address to his countrymen before his speech to the Australian parliament. Xi laid out plans to make China a global superpower through economic, military and technological might. The strategy would be "building a socialism that is superior to capitalism, and laying the foundation for a future where we will win the initiative and have the dominant position." So while publicly promising sincerity and trust, Xi secretly sought to bully his partners with all the money that China had gained with its one-sided relationship with western nations. "Made in China" now meant "huge profits made by the CCP state-controlled economy spent on military weapons."

The first forays against Oz came via cyberattacks, with Chinese state-linked terrorists hacking the Australian parliament, the country's Bureau of Meteorology, the Australian National University, attacks on Australia's Chinese-language media, along with coercion and intimidation on any outlet daring to depart from the CCP hard line.

News emerged that China had secretly invested with some of the Australian political establishment by demanding policy in China's favor. Beijing-linked businesses were the largest sources of donations with foreign ties, and the money went to both sides of the political spectrum. When discovered, the bribery shook up Australian politics. In 2017, Australian Labour Party Senator Sam Dastyari was forced to resign over his ties to Chinese Communist Party-linked donors.

Then China hit Australia with a series of trade restrictions and tariffs in response to Canberra's call for an independent investigation into the origins of the coronavirus pandemic, which had reportedly emerged from the Chinese city of Wuhan. Meanwhile, China was also building its military bases in the South China Sea, plus eliminating democratic rights in Hong Kong and threatening an invasion of Taiwan, moving southward militarily toward Australia.

In 2021 Canberra announced its wide-ranging security partnership with the U.S. and U.K. The pact, dubbed AUKUS, comes amid a broader Australian attempt to turn away from China. "The level of Chinese economic coercion and cyber espionage against Australia was once unimaginable, so our security agencies have learned to consider worst-case possibilities," said Rory Medcalf, head of the National Security College at the Australian National University. Under the new Anglo-American alliance, the U.S., U.K. and Australia have agreed to share advanced technologies with one another, including artificial intelligence, cybersecurity, quantum computing, underwater systems and long-range strike capabilities.

The Australian government is considering stripping a Chinese company of its 99-year lease of the strategically crucial Port of Darwin. Meanwhile U.S. Marines regularly rotate through Darwin for training exercises, and Australia's Defense Minister has proposed expanding their numbers and forming a joint training brigade with Australian troops. He warned Canberra must be prepared for whatever lurks "on or below the horizon" amid growing tensions with China.

On my way back to the airport my limo driver inquires as to my profession. When I tell him I am a travel writer, he points to the lush trees lining each side of the highway, proof positive that Cairns is located in a rainforest. Do I know what those black shapes are in the trees, hiding in the foliage? Yes, I replied, I did. I had been notified on arrival that the black shapes were fruit bats, sleeping all day and then waking at dusk to fly into the jungle in search of food. The massive hordes of bats blackened the skies like a Dracula movie. I had been warned by my earlier limo driver that if I wished to shoot photos or video footage of the fantastic display, it might be better to do so while under cover, if I caught his drift. Yes, I said, the naïve and innocent often get shit upon through their own ignorance, so always best to keep a sharp eye out when you don't know what the hell is going on.

SKULL AND BONES

It's always interesting to discover how some people rise to places of power and prominence based on their family's wealth, and how that family became rich in the first place. The Kennedy clan, it is well known, became rich as rum runners during prohibition, alcohol being illegal at the time but no longer. Using an inheritance, Fred Trump built and managed property in New York City. Trump Senior was investigated by a U.S. Senate committee for profiteering in 1954 but not jailed, and again by the State of New York in 1966. In the mid-1970s, his son "The Donald" received loans from his father exceeding $14 million. But it is the Bush family empire that intrigues. You see, it was George W. Bush's grandfather who helped Hitler's rise to power.

The late U.S. senator Prescott Bush was a director and shareholder of companies that profited from their involvement with the financial backers of Nazi Germany. Bush's business dealings, which continued until his company's assets were seized in 1942 under the Trading with the Enemy Act, led more than 60 years later to a civil action for damages being brought in Germany against the Bush family by two former slave laborers at Auschwitz. The evidence also prompted one former U.S. Nazi war crimes prosecutor to argue that the late senator's action should have been grounds for his prosecution for giving aid and comfort to the enemy.

Documents finally declassified show that even after America had entered the war, and when there was already significant information about the Nazis' plans and policies, Bush worked for and profited from companies closely involved with the very German businesses that financed Hitler's rise to power. It has also been noted that the money he made from these dealings helped to establish the Bush family fortune and set up its political dynasty.

Prescott Bush, a 6-ft 4-inch charmer with a rich singing voice, was the founder of the Bush political dynasty and was once considered a potential Presidential candidate himself. Like his son, George, and grandson, George W, he went to Yale where he was, like his descendants, a member of the secretive and influential Skull and Bones senior society. He was an artillery captain and involved with the intelligence services in the First World War. After the U.S. sent George H.W. Bush to China in October of 1974, his brother Prescott Jr., founder of the United States-China Chamber of Commerce, went to Shanghai in the early 1980s and started to hand-out the money to build all the gulag factories that launched the Chinese economic revival. Both were members of The Order of Skull & Bones. One wonders where all this money came from? Eventually we will discover some came from "Yamashita's Gold," but more on that later.

So what the heck is Skull and Bones anyway? According to Wikipedia, Skull and Bones, also known as The Order, Order Chapter 322 or The

Brotherhood of Death, is an undergraduate senior secret student society at Yale University in New Haven, Connecticut. The oldest senior class society at the university, Skull and Bones has become a cultural institution known for its powerful alumni and the various conspiracy theories about this "secret society."

Skull and Bones membership developed a reputation for being only for the "power elite." Like other Yale senior societies, Skull and Bones membership was almost exclusively limited to white Protestant males. While Yale itself had exclusionary policies directed at particular ethnic and religious groups, the senior societies were even more exclusionary. Skull and Bones even had a reputation for stealing keepsakes from other Yale societies or from campus buildings; society members reportedly call the practice "crooking" and strived to outdo each other's "crooks." The group Skull and Bones has been featured in several books and movies which claim that the society plays a key role in a "global conspiracy for world control."

However, the January 1990 issue of *The New Federalist* reveals much more about the Bush family's wealth and history. In an article titled "Bush's China Policy is Skull and Bones," Joseph Brewda wrote the following history. "An obscure secret society may have more to do with George Bush's obsessive support of Beijing's mass murderers than one may think. Skull and Bones is a secret fraternity at Yale University which is restricted to a mere fifteen student members per year. The society was formed in 1832 by General William Russell, whose family's shipping firm dominated the U.S. side of the China opium trade. Yale University was founded by Eli Yale, who made his fortune working for the opium smuggling British East India Company."

George H.W. Bush, Siva Yam, President of USCCC, and Prescott Bush, Founder of USCCC

53

Skull and Bones became the recruiting grounds and preserve of the most important New England families who also made their fortunes in the drug trade. They are a dominant element of the U.S. Eastern Establishment to this day. George H.W. Bush, the second U.S. diplomatic representative to the People's Republic of China back in 1974, was a member of Skull and Bones. So were his father, brother, son, uncle, nephew, and several cousins. Winston Lord, the Reagan-Bush administration Ambassador to China was a member; so were his father and several other relatives. James Lilley, an Ambassador to China, had been an early CIA operative. Many of U.S. Ambassador to Beijing since Kissinger's secret deal with Mao Zedong have been Yalies. A mere coincidence?

Back in 1903, Yale Divinity School established a number of schools and hospitals throughout China that were collectively known as Yale in China. It has since been shown that Yale in China was an intelligence network whose purpose was to destroy the Republican movement of Sun Yat-sen on behalf of the Anglo-American Establishment. They hated Yat-sen because he wanted to modernize China. On the other hand, they loved the Chinese communists because they were committed to keep growing dope. One of Yale in China's most important associates was Mao Zedong.

During World War II, Yale in China was a primary instrument used by the U.S. Establishment and its Office of Strategic Services (OSS) to install the Maoists into power. Yale in China was run by OSS operative Reuben Holden, the husband of Bush's cousin, and also a member of Skull and Bones. The Maoists made China into the world's largest opium producer. Mao created and supported by the CIA? Opium the source of wealth for the American elite? Who knew? Let's go back to Wikipedia again and see what it has to say about the opium trade in China.

Mao Zedong rented part of Yale-in-China's former medical clinic in 1919.

"The history of opium in China began with the use of opium for medicinal purposes during the 7th century. In the 17th century the practice of mixing opium with tobacco for smoking spread from Southeast Asia, creating a far greater demand. The decade of the 1830s witnessed a rapid rise in opium trade, and by 1838, just before the First Opium War, it had climbed to 40,000 chests. The rise continued on after the Treaty of Nanking (1842) that concluded the war. By 1858 annual imports had risen to 70,000 chests."

By the late 19th century Chinese domestic opium production challenged and then surpassed imports. The 20th century opened with effective campaigns to suppress domestic farming, and in 1907 the British government signed a treaty to eliminate imports. The fall of the Qing dynasty in 1911, however, led to resurgence in domestic production. The Nationalist Government, provincial governments, the revolutionary bases of the Chinese Communist Party (CCP), and the British colonial government of Hong Kong all depended on opium taxes as major sources of revenue, as did the Japanese occupation governments during the Second Sino-Japanese War (1937-45). After 1949, both the respective governments of the People's Republic of China on the mainland and of the Republic of China on Taiwan claimed to have successfully suppressed the widespread growth and use of opium. In fact, opium products were still in production in Xinjiang and Northeast China.

An online article by reporter James Corbett in October, 2011 describes the long involvement of the CIA in the drug trade. He wrote that the cultivation of what we know today as the opium poppy goes back to the beginnings of recorded history, when the Sumerians in ancient Mesopotamia cultivated what they referred to as Hul Gil, or the "joy plant." The practice was passed down through the Assyrians to the Babylonians and to the Egyptians, by which time the opium trade was becoming a lynchpin of international trade across the Mediterranean into Europe.

During the 18th century, the British monopolized the opium trade in India and shipped thousands of chests of opium per year to China from India as a way of financing their huge trade deficit with that nation. When the Chinese cracked down on opium trafficking in the mid-19th century, the British fought two wars to ensure their Chinese opium market. By the 1830s, American traders got in on the act, with "Russell & Company" becoming the largest American trading house in China. Samuel Russell's cousin, William Russell, co-founded Skull & Bones, the secret society at Yale that formed the core of the American intelligence establishment in China.

Just as the British Empire was in part financed by their control of the opium trade through the British East India Company, so too has the CIA been found time after time to be at the heart of the modern international drug trade. From its very inception, the CIA has been embroiled in the murky underworld of drug trafficking. In the late 1940s, the CIA funneled arms and funds to the Corsican Mafia in return for their assistance in breaking up widespread labor strikes in France. The Corsican crime syndicate, in turn, used the CIA support to set up the trafficking network known as "The French Connection" which saw heroin smuggled from Turkey to France, and then shipped to the U.S. and launching an American heroin epidemic.

In Burma in 1950, the CIA regrouped the remnants of the defeated Nationalist Chinese Army, or KMT, to start an invasion of Southern China and draw Chinese troops away from the Korean front. Easily beaten back by Mao's forces, the KMT instead turned their attention to occupying Burma, imposing an opium tax on all farmers in the opium-rich Shan highlands. The KMT opium was flown out to Thailand and Taiwan in the same unmarked C-47s that the CIA had used to supply the group in the first place.

In the 1960s and early 1970s, the CIA recruited the Laotian Hmong tribe to fight communist forces in the region. The CIA encouraged the Hmong to grow opium instead of rice to make them dependent on CIA air drops of food. The agency then forced compliance by threatening to withdraw the food aid. To make the deal even sweeter, they even located a heroin refinery at CIA headquarters in northern Laos and used Air America, a passenger and cargo airline that was covertly owned and operated by the CIA, to export the Laotian opium and heroin. Much of it ended up in Vietnam, causing an epidemic of heroin addiction in U.S. soldiers.

In the 1980s, the U.S. supported the Contras in their fight against the Sandinista government in Nicaragua. Officially barred from arming and funding the Contras by Congress, the CIA came up with a scheme to sell arms to Iran and use the funds to illegally arm and supply the Contras. CIA-protected drug smugglers flew down to Nicaragua loaded with arms to supply the Contras and flew back loaded with Columbian cocaine, the beginning of the crack epidemic in America. Despite the numerous, documented and fully admitted examples of CIA involvement in drug dealing in the past, the idea that the agency is still tied in with international drug traffickers is largely dismissed as the stuff of conspiracy theory.

After the publication of an exposé on the CIA-Contra drug connections in the *San Jose Mercury News* in 1996, reporter Gary Webb was subjected to fierce critiques. The backlash eventually forced Webb's editors at the *Mercury News* to back away from the story. The CIA's own internal investigation by Inspector General Frederick Hitz vindicated much of Webb's reporting, but Webb remained a journalistic outcast and his story was commonly believed to be discredited. In 2004, Webb was found dead from two gunshot wounds to the head – the death was ruled a suicide.

In late 2009, Antonio Maria Costa, the head of the United Nations Office on Drugs and Crime, went on record to say that it was primarily drug

THE LAND OF OZ

money that kept the American financial system afloat during the 2008 crisis, estimating that some $352 billion dollars of drug profits had been laundered via the major U.S. banks during that time.

From the book jacket of a current bestseller comes corroborating evidence that some of the American "elite," if you can call them that, may have been secretly working with the Chinese Communist Party. In his book *Red-Handed: How American Elites Get Rich Helping China Win*, a #1 New York Times bestseller, Peter Schweizer says that as an investigative journalist this is the scariest investigation he has ever conducted. That the Chinese government seeks to infiltrate American institutions is hardly surprising, he says. What is wholly new, however, are the number of American elites who are eager to help the Chinese dictatorship in its quest for global hegemony. Presidential families, Silicon Valley gurus, Wall Street high rollers, Ivy League universities, even professional athletes – all willing to sacrifice American strength and security on the altar of personal enrichment. Schweizer goes so far as to say that many of these elites quietly believe the Chinese dictatorial regime is superior to American democracy.

CHAPTER SIX

CHINA: THE DRAGON EMERGES

Oxford dictionary: Communism is a political theory derived from Karl Marx, advocating class war and leading to a society in which all property is publicly owned and each person works and is paid according to their abilities and needs.

Anyone who has been there knows that Hong Kong is not the "real China," although the Chinese Communist Party under the command of dictator Xi Jinping seems determined to strip the city of the freedoms that make it different from mainland China and so turn Hong Kong into another subservient vassal state. Anyone who has been to Hong Kong will quickly realize that the city is one of the most expensive places in the world and therefore should arrange their hotel accommodations accordingly. On my many trips through Hong Kong I have never enjoyed the luxury of being "comped," (i.e. treated to a complimentary visit by the Tourism Bureau), so unfortunately today I have to pay the freight myself. In which case I can either sleep on a bench at the airport with a suitcase locked to my wrist, or find a cheap hotel in Kowloon across the bay.

The metropolitan area encompassing Hong Kong, Kowloon, Shenzhen and Guangdong (formerly known as Canton) has a population of over 50 million people. The Mong Kok neighborhood of Kowloon boasts an extremely high population of 340,000 residents per square mile, described as the "densest district in the world" by the Guinness Book of Records, so online I have booked a room in the Dragon Inn in Mong Kok. Located on the 22nd floor of an old and decrepit concrete office tower, the Dragon proves to be virtually empty as I arrive late at night after a long flight from North America. A small room with a small light bulb in a dark corridor reveals an old man reading a newspaper who hands me the key to my room without saying a word, and I shuffle down the dark corridor and along several hallways until I come to my room, which apparently has been renovated from being a broom closest into a hotel room simply by somehow inserting a bed into the available space. I measure the room for posterity; it is 37 inches wide and 72 inches long. How anyone managed to stuff a bed into it is another mystery, but for $24 U.S. in Hong Kong you don't get a master bedroom with ensuite facilities and a view.

In the morning I discover that the elevator doesn't work so I walk down 22 flights of stairs to the lobby with my bag, but the door is locked, so I descend further to the basement which turns out to be full of parked cars, climb on to the hood of one car, and slither through a window to the outside world, where I discover approximately five million people commuting to work, somewhat like a rock concert without the music. Carried afloat by the masses, I manage to find the subway and make my way to the Star Ferry on the western side of Hong Kong bay, perhaps the cheapest tourist attraction in the world, the fare of five cents not having increased since the ferry was first built many decades ago. I grab a seat and enjoy the fabulous view of the downtown Hong Kong skyscrapers crawling up the hill towards Victoria Peak. A funicular tram line that serves as a tourist attraction crawls up towards Victoria Peak at the top, but for those on an economy budget the free alternative is simply to wait until the Central-Midlevel Escalator reverses flow.

This is the longest outdoor covered escalator system in the world. The system covers 2,600 feet in distance and traverses an elevation of over 443 feet in over a dozen different sections from bottom to top. In the morning commute it descends until 10 A.M., then reverses flow and takes tourists and people doing business uphill. There are restaurants and other tourist attractions along the way for those travelers lucky enough to know of the escalators' existence. I shoot photos and video all along the way, pausing at the top to take a photo of the sign (in English) stating "no video allowed," which I think should better be placed at the bottom but what do I know? It's a lovely walk downhill. It is extremely depressing to think that this fabulous cosmopolitan city has fallen under the harsh thumb of Mao's successors, who will likely eliminate any democratic adversaries brave enough to resist communist doctrine that demands extreme obedience.

Anyone attempting to visit any region of China is well advised to fly directly to a major city and switch to a train. If you want to see what 1.2 billion people look like up close you can take a bus. Today I am doing just that, taking a shuttle from the airport to Szhenzen on the western shores of the bay, and then transferring to a "sleeper bus" on my journey to Yangshuo in Guilin province. Not that long ago Shenzhen was a sleepy little fishing village; now there are 10 million people living in new high rise buildings that stretch endlessly from the shoreline for many miles inland. It's incredible how China has changed and I cannot comprehend how many billions of dollars were required to build thousands of new high rise towers.

It's easy to say that China is no longer communist, ha ha. At the border crossing a huge sign in English encourages any travelers with complaints or questions to push a red button. The button is the size of a large pizza. "Go ahead, press the button," says my photographer Brian. "Ask a question. Make a complaint."

"No one has ever pressed that button," I reply grimly, "and no one ever will. There isn't a single finger print on it. If you press that button a giant hole opens in the ground and you disappear, never to be seen again."

We arrive at the Shenzhen bus station. There isn't a single syllable of English to be found anywhere, on the walls or even on the onward bus tickets we buy. We have already entered new territory, well off the tourist trail. This is the first and last time I have ever used a sleeper bus and for good reason. Anyone over five feet is considered tall in China and those of us over six feet tall will experience difficulties such as attempting to sleep with your knees jammed into your face. In this instance I am accompanied by my photographer carrying two large duffle bags who complains so vociferously about my chosen mode of transport that I drift off to sleep listening to the endless drone.

Thanks to *Lonely Planet*, the little town of Yangshuo in Guilin province has been "discovered" and has become a must for western backpackers traveling the Asian backpacker circuit. The region's topography of bizarre toadstool-shaped mountains, winding rivers, lush green fields, massive caves, creeks on which to raft, biking trails and the town's vibrant downtown with bars and restaurants all make a visit very pleasurable. As with all my trips I have done advance research and booked a room at the White Lion Hotel, mainly because the small print on its website revealed that its American owner Jeffrey Powell donates all the hotel's profits to the local school board, buying and distributing text books as a form of philanthropy. As luck would have it, Jeffrey is in town and in the process of planning visits to several schools and I am invited to join him and his girlfriend Anna on the trips.

After having just been in Taiwan, I am astonished at the difference between the two countries. Both Mao and Chiang Kai-shek insisted there was only one China and they were the ruler of it, but that was many years ago. Taiwan has obviously gone an entirely different direction from the Mainland. Its streets are immaculate, its people are modern and polite, the culture is civilized and everything is very high tech. I learn my lesson quickly that the Chinese Mainland is different just by trying to cross the street in Yangshuo at a marked pedestrian crosswalk on a green light. The vehicular traffic doesn't even slow down. I am reminded of India, where (just like in a knife fight) the first rule is: "There are no rules." In Yangshuo pedestrians have no rights at all except on the appropriately named West Street, the main thoroughfare and tourist attraction with lots of consumer shops and restaurants. No vehicles are allowed on West Street so as to keep the mortality rate low, but even on West Street most Chinese people spit on the ground and evidence poor manners such as pushing and shoving, and tourists are well advised to carry their backpacks on the front and not the back for fear of theft.

As a tourist town Yangshuo offers such western delights as Kentucky Fried Chicken and McDonalds. I always go to a Golden Arches on all my trips, certainly not to eat there but to take photos of the menu boards to witness whatever fast foods are on offer and at what prices. This has worked well as a storyline everywhere I have traveled except Zurich, where the manager had the eyes of a hawk and spotted me and my camera and immediately blocked me from entering. So you will have to take my word that a Big Mac in Switzerland costs more than a used car in North America, and that's with no fries or a coke. But it is in Yangshuo in a

West Street in Yangshuo, Guilin province is named after all the western tourists who flock to the region for its spectacularblandscape and outdoor activities.

Szechuan restaurant, chowing down on chili peppered dishes hot enough to cause flames to emit from your nose, that I get my first introduction to Chinese communism.

It is a busy restaurant. The Chinese don't love to eat, they live to eat. The room is packed and the noise levels are high. Nonetheless I can hear very loud shouting emanating from the other side of the restaurant, and witness a man standing on the top of a table tap dancing between the dishes and shouting at the top of his voice. Red-faced and hoarse, he is obviously roaring drunk. I turn and ask one of the Chinese people in our party why the drunk isn't escorted from the premises or pitched headlong down the stairs. The answer is given in a whisper.

"He's a cadre. They are all cadres at that table."

"What," I ask in my stupidity, "is a cadre?"

"Keep your voice down," he replies in a whisper. "They are Communist Party members. They can do whatever they want. Don't say or do anything."

My friend, as it turns out, is a member of a local ethnic minority, a so-called "hill tribe." There are several hill tribes in the region and they are apparently not fond of the all-powerful Han majority. I get a quick rundown. China is composed of 56 ethnic groups. Among them the Han Chinese account for 92 percent of the overall Chinese population and the other 55 make up the remaining 8 percent. With a population of 1.2 billion, the Han Chinese can be found in almost every part of China. However, they mainly live in the middle and lower reaches of the Yellow River, Yangtze River and the Pearl River, and also in the Northeast Plain Region. They form the largest ethnic group within China and are also the largest ethnic group in the world.

The CCP is the sole governing party of the People's Republic and its membership is 95 million, representing only 7 percent of the Chinese population. Therefore, says my informant, only a small percentage of the Chinese people are Communists and "everybody hates them." Given there are 95 million people in the Party I don't plan to take a survey, but I am surprised to learn only a small proportion of the Chinese population is Communist. Hey, I thought everyone in China was a Communist. According to my friend, the Han majority, and especially the CCP, oppresses ethnic minorities in a wide variety of ways, like with forced sterilization and the concentration camps imposed on the Muslim population of Xinjiang in western China.

My ignorance of China is profound in many ways, I admit to him, but I make a mental note not to offend any Communist Party members I happen to meet on my trip, a strategy that comes in very handy the following day. Jeffrey announces that he and Anna are going to visit three different schools and hand out books and awards and would I like to tag along? There is a vehicle waiting outside but to Jeffrey's surprise it is not the vehicle he ordered. In fact, it is a spanking new mini-van with a driver at the wheel, a woman with a business suit in the passenger seat, and a man with a large TV camera in the second row of seats. Upon investigation it turns out that the woman is a CCP cadre, and she has brought along a cameraman to shoot video footage of the day's proceedings. How she knew that Jeffrey was going to visit schools remains a mystery to him, and I would certainly like to know if she is aware that I am a journalist and, if so, how she found out. My visa application says "retired," because I know better than to put "journalist" on any visa application. My heart is in my mouth as we leave.

It is a long drive north of Yangshuo on a poorly paved two-lane highway, then an hour bouncing down a rough dirt road to the village. It is hot enough to cook outside without using an oven. The air itself is an oven. The cadre sits in the front seat jabbering into her cellphone and the rest of us sit in the back and keep our mouths shut. It is a brand new van with excellent air conditioning and a five-speed fan that blows hard enough to put a part in your hair. Inside the van it is quite pleasant. Outside, not so much. There are no stops along the way because no one wants to get out of the van in the heat. The last hour is rather nasty and I can see the cadre starting to get upset. She is wearing a suit, somewhat inappropriate given the fact we are in the jungle, and her hair is getting messed up from the indoor typhoon. The heat is actually not an issue as long as you don't wind down a window, which I don't try a second time.

We finally arrive at the nameless village that is our destination. Rather, we almost arrive but the road is blocked by a very large dump of bricks. It appears that the village is building a large structure of some sort, and the trucks delivering the bricks had simply dumped them all on the dirt road, effectively blocking the path. I don't count them all but I estimate there are a few million. An old man in a straw hat and yellow sandals is attempting to pile the bricks to one side of the road, and given the speed at which he is going and the heat in which he is working, I estimate it will take a decade until he is finished, if he doesn't die first.

In order to expedite matters the cadre leans over and gives a good long blast on the horn, which startles the old man into hasty action. Instead of picking one brick at a time, he picks up two and gives them a good toss. I can see his problem right away. He is attempting to toss them all on to the right side of the road and not the left as well, which probably annoys the Communist cadre. Inside the van all conversation comes to a halt. There is no way we can pass until all the bricks are moved. The cadre is now red in the face. She no doubt has a strict schedule to follow, prisoners to execute, townsfolk to browbeat, and taxes to collect. She winds down the window on the passenger side of the car to give the old man a verbal blast but immediately winds the window back up again so she doesn't catch on fire. Then she digs out her phone and starts dialing. I don't speak a word of Chinese but I get the distinct impress she is calling the army or police and arranging to have the old man shot.

As a Canadian, I understand there is a simple solution to the conundrum. We Canucks may be used to the cold, but we aren't a lazy bunch even when it's red hot, so to speak. While everyone in the van sits and stews and complains, I simply get out of the vehicle and go to help the old man move the bricks. Initially I point out to him that there are two sides to every argument and we might as well toss the bricks on both sides of the road, because he is building Mt. Everest on the right and will soon need a ladder. This strategy had not apparently occurred to him, but I had already ascertained during my short time in the region that everything in China is done to the left, if you catch my drift. And so it went. I toss my bricks like a demon because I don't want him shot while I am still in the

The author, left, helps an elderly villager in a remote jungle town in Guilin to clear the road of a delivery of bricks.

vicinity, and in a jiffy (well, longer than that) we clear a path for the van to proceed.

We meet a young man and his family, and Jeffrey awards him a scholarship and the government agent poses for a photo with the young man in order to get the official credit, and we then return to a middle school in Yangshuo and hand out books, and then a high school in Yangshuo where the same BS occurs. The CCP videographer shoots footage and I am amazed to be sitting in the bar of the White Lion nursing a cold beer when the footage is shown on the TV on the six o'clock news. Happily, I am edited out of the coverage and there is no mention of my pile of bricks. The government cadre takes all the credit for the awards and Jeffrey doesn't mind that at all. I think he regards the CCP interference as a form of "protection" from a shakedown by the local mafia. I never did learn what they were going to do with all those damned bricks.

The local's fear of the CCP reminds me to do some research, especially on long-dead Chairman Mao. Wikipedia describes Mao Zedong (December 26, 1893 - September 9, 1976), also known as Chairman Mao, as "a Chinese communist revolutionary who was the founding father of the People's Republic of China, which he ruled as the chairman of the Chinese Communist Party (CCP) from the establishment of the PRC in 1949 until his death in 1976." To this day Mao is still seen as the Great Leader in China, the greatest hero in the history of the country. His portrait remains on walls and desks everywhere. That's the short story. As I do my research, the real history is somewhat longer and far more violent.

Despite his reputation being totally whitewashed over the years, I soon deduce Mao was probably the biggest mass murderer in the history of mankind. Most people probably think that Adolf Hitler, architect of the Holocaust, was the greatest murderer because he killed so many people in enemy countries. (We are referring to modern mass murderers; Genghis Khan and Alexander the Great killed a huge number of people on their conquests but that was long ago.) You might also mention former Soviet dictator Joseph Stalin, who managed to kill even more innocent people than Hitler did, during Stalin's terror regime that likely took more lives than the Holocaust, but both Hitler and Stalin were outdone in sheer numbers by the psychopathic madman Mao Zedong.

According to many reports from modern psychologists, Mao suffered from multiple personality disorder, exhibiting psycho-pathology, narcissistic personality disorder and paranoid personality disorder. He also derived great pleasure from stirring up extreme violence. His plan for China

66

Although Communist Party founder Mao Zedong killed millions of his own people through The Great Leap Forward and the Cultural Revolution his memory is still used to intimidate Chinese citizens into obedience.

was a direct reflection of this potent mix of psycho-pathology. Like the visions of other psychopathic leaders, including Hitler, Stalin and Pol Pot, Mao's vision for China was essentially a simplistic, narcissistic fantasy. The ideology of communism, with its promises of equality, an end to worker exploitation, and a future society based on justice, provided the propaganda cover that Mao needed to rise to power.

After grabbing control of the CCP in 1949, from 1958 to 1962 Mao's Great Leap Forward policy led to the deaths of up to 45 million people, the biggest episode of mass murder ever recorded. Of particular interest is the fact that the people he killed were his own. In the interests of "modernization," Mao herded villagers all across the country into giant people's communes. In pursuit of a utopian paradise, everything was "collectivized." People had their work, homes, land, belongings and livelihoods stolen from them and given to the Party.

Food was distributed by the spoonful according to "merit," a point system based on his own nasty idea that food could be used as a weapon to force people to follow the Party's ideology. As incentives to work were destroyed, coercion and violence were used to force famished farmers to perform labor on poorly planned irrigation projects while their own fields were neglected. Remember the old joke about Communism? "We pretend to work and they pretend to pay us."

By the late spring of 1958 in China collective farms were becoming mandatory. Rural cadres began to amalgamate as many as 20 neighboring villages to form a single integrated administrative unit, with populations as high as 20,000 people. All over China, rural officials rushed to emulate the idea. Extraordinary claims of unprecedented crop yields began to appear in the Party's propaganda. Why, the summer wheat harvest in 1958 was said to have virtually doubled from the previous year! New breakthroughs in productivity were reported almost daily as rural officials across the country competed to meet and exceed established norms of per-acre production. The communes could, it was argued, become entirely self-sufficient, not merely in food production but in industry, commerce, education, and military training as well! No longer bound by the conventional technocratic constraints of the old Soviet communism model, China was blazing a new and original pathway to the future!

Perhaps the most famous example of rural economic diversification during the Great Leap Forward was the campaign to somehow create large amounts of high-quality steel in backyard blast furnaces. Mao declared that his goal was to surpass Great Britain in steel production within 15 years. Throughout the countryside, millions of peasants were conscripted to build small-scale clay or brick-and-mortar kilns. To keep the furnaces blazing, all available rural fuel supplies were consumed. Whole forests were denuded of trees, and all available household heating and cooking coal were requisitioned. Scrap metal was collected in every village, including old farm tools, bicycle parts, household pots, pans, forks and spoons, and even family woks.

By the end of 1958 the country's 750,000 collective farms had been consolidated and merged into just 23,000 people's communes. In the excitement of the moment, it escaped notice that most of the communes had been set up without much planning or preparation. This didn't stop the Party's propagandists from proclaiming unprecedented breakthroughs from steelmaking and grain production to medical science and even athletic competition.

As it turned out, however, most backyard furnaces were only capable of producing pig iron and the propaganda about huge increases in food production was just that – propaganda. Personal farms were left to rot. Millions of people starved to death. Aside from mass starvation, up to three million victims were tortured to death or executed, often for the slightest infraction. The Party kept detailed records of its own horrors. When a starving boy stole a handful of grain in a Hunan village, the Party forced his father to bury him alive. A starving farmer was reported to the central leadership for stealing a potato so one of his ears was chopped off, his legs were tied with iron wire, and he was marked with a branding iron. People were executed just for complaining about starving. Insane dictator Pol Pot copied the same methods later in Cambodia, encouraging children to murder their parents so the country could start as new from the Year Zero.

While the horrors of the Great Leap Forward are still well known to history experts, most ordinary people in the western world have never heard of the catastrophe. This is because the victims were simple Chinese peasants, far away and unimportant. In recent years the CCP has admitted that Mao made "mistakes," as if starving tens of millions of people to death on purpose didn't prove that communism as an ideology doesn't function in real life. The Party is unwilling to discuss that Mao's mass murdering was intentional and continues to persecute dissidents who point out the truth. The obvious reason is that the Communist Party still rules China with an iron fist, just as Mao did, and the current regime under Xi Jinping still derives much of its power from the fact that they can kill as many people as they want and no one can do anything about it. Similar grandiose plans like the Great Leap Forward could possibly be revived in the future if the Party thinks such methods are necessary for the Party to survive.

I enjoy my time exploring Guilin District except for the fact that the sky doesn't exist. It has been conscripted into the ideology and disappeared. Even here in Guilin, far away from those manufacturing regions where the pollution is so thick you can cut it with a knife and insert into a blast furnace, the skies are full of soot. I cough up dirt after biking or hiking. My photographer is upset; good photos are impossible to find. The people in Yangshuo are friendly and the food is decent and cheap. I am approached by two young teenage girls who want to practice their English. I am well known as a great spender and splash out generously; our meal of noodles and tea costs me almost a dollar.

The girls are delighted when they discover I am Canadian. They explain most English speaking people here are Australian and the Aussie pronunciation of English is weird. The Aussie backpackers are offered free room and board and beer at schools if they will simply stay for a few weeks and talk to students over beers. Knowing the Aussies, I can see why this proposal has proved a great success. I am tempted to extend my holiday and teach English. The girls tell me they had to apply for a permit to take the bus to Yangshuo from their village in the country. To them, China is the entire world. They have no plans to travel overseas, but they are curious to know what the world is like. They have no opinions about communism. They are unaware that in the rest of the world there are multiple and often opposing political options. In China, you can vote for anyone you want, as long as you vote communist.

Having already enjoyed the opportunity to travel via sleeper bus, I choose to return to Hong Kong via plane. It's a long bus ride west to the city of Guilin and its airport. I am exhausted by several weeks of non-stop adventures and travel and I struggle to stay awake on the bus. I collapse on my seat on the plane but decide to have a quick peek at some of the thousands of photos I have taken. The camera case is empty. An expert thief has somehow stolen my precious Panasonic Lumix that I love so dearly. Thankfully I had already removed the memory chips. I wonder what the punishment for such a theft would be in modern China. Capital punishment? In a country where simply objecting to the government can get you thrown in prison, I am happy to be going home.

U.S. CHINA TRADE HISTORY

A few years ago, I published this OpEd in The Vancouver Sun.

In 1980, the U.S. Congress passed a trade agreement conferring Most Favored Nation status on China. This exempted Chinese exports to the United States from high tariff rates stipulated by the Smoot-Hawley Act of June 1930. Immediately U.S. consumer goods corporations were drawn to China by the lure of very low wages and vast profits. First to the fray were corporate brands such as H. J. Heinz, R. J. Reynolds Tobacco, Coca-Cola, American Express, American Motors, General Foods, Gillette, Pepsi-Cola, Eastman Kodak, AT&T, Nabisco, and Bell South. Over time, American companies lowered their costs of manufacturing by 87 percent. Since that time, annual average wages for blue and white collar jobs in North America have decreased 10 percent, while income for the top corporate executives who designed the scheme have risen 970 percent. The average wage for a top American corporate executive is now $16 million.

China and America became huge trade partners. Today America buys endless amounts of cheap consumer goods from China, which lends its profits back by purchasing U.S. Treasury bills. China is now the largest foreign holder of U.S. Treasury notes, allowing the United States to maintain a massive budgetary deficit. China owns over $1.2 trillion in American debt out of total U.S. debt of $16 trillion (more than 100 percent of U.S. GDP.) A few years ago figures from both countries show that American global trade is currently worth US$3.82 trillion, while China's total trade is US$3.87 trillion, so China now exceeds the United States as the world's largest trading nation. Thanks to the historic 1972 Nixon trade visit, designed to paint him as a global statesman and perhaps deflect public attention from the Watergate burglary, many economists predict that the Chinese economy will become twice as big as the United States by 2030.

The current U.S. trade deficit with China has been verified by many economists as "the largest ever recorded with a single economy in global history." China is more than happy to own a large portion of U.S. debt because buying U.S. Treasury notes helps China keep its own currency weaker than the dollar. This keeps products exported from China cheaper than U.S. products, creating millions of jobs for the Chinese people. The U.S. allowed China to become its biggest banker because North Americans have become seriously addicted to consumerism as a lifestyle and want their goods. Selling debt to China keeps U.S. interest rates low. However, China's ownership of U.S. debt is shifting the economic and political balance of global power massively in China's favor.

A blue-footed booby on Espanola Island in the Galapagos stares at the author with an innocent face, unafraid of humans.

CHAPTER SEVEN

DARWIN AND THE
THEORY OF EVOLUTION

We are in danger of destroying ourselves by our greed and stupidity. We cannot remain looking inwards at ourselves on a small and increasingly polluted and overcrowded planet.

- Stephen Hawking

The remote island of Espanola in the Galapagos is a strange place to learn about the real meaning of the phrase "survival of the fittest." The plane from Guayaquil, Ecuador lands at Puerto Baquerizo Moreno airport on the island of San Christobal where passengers take a shuttle to the harbor and board a zodiac to transfer to the *MV Grace*, a fancy wooden yacht. If you are going to explore the Galapagos, I would recommend a vessel like the *Grace*. Built by billionaire Greek shipping magnate Aristotle Onassis who gave it to Princess Grace of Monaco on the occasion of her marriage to the Prince of Monaco, the sleek luxury yacht has somehow ended up here in the far nether regions of the world to accommodate and transfer passengers from island to island in one of the most unique locations on the planet. Unlike a big cruise ship, there are only a dozen passengers and a guide, which makes all the difference when getting an education about the Galapagos wildlife, as I most certainly do.

Being a travel writer from North America whose articles will be published in many Canadian newspapers, I am offered a complimentary voyage by the Ecuadorian Tourism Bureau. This contrasts sharply with the rather large sums of money forked out by the other paying customers to enjoy a "once in a lifetime adventure," but to balance the books I am given a berth in the bottom of the boat with only a porthole for a view. As it surprisingly turns out, there are three decks on the yacht and the higher up the berth the more subject that berth is to wave action, so the honeymooners on the top deck get pitched around like softballs every night. The second surprise is that the yacht transfers between islands at night so you need to be roped into your berth as you sleep in order to avoid being tossed onto the floor.

The third and far more pleasant surprise is discovered over breakfast the next morning as naturalist and guide Rafael Pesantes, a world class ornithologist, explains the rules of the game. It takes six generations for the "fear gene" to grow within the animal brain. The animals on the Galapagos, except for the giant tortoises on the main island of Santa Cruz that were captured by whaling crews for food on long ocean journeys, have never been attacked or exploited by human beings. Therefore the birds and marine mammals are not afraid of tourists, no matter how badly dressed we may be. The islands belong to them; we are merely short term lookie-loos. Under no circumstances whatsoever, says Rafael, are we to harass the wildlife or step off the path. Look, take photos, but do not approach. Likely all the creatures we meet will simply ignore our intrusion, he says, but watch out for the alpha male sea lions on the beach that will protect their harems.

This news about the animals being "tame" (which is not the right word) comes as quite a surprise. There are many reasons why tourists spend a fortune to come all the way to this collection of barren rocks in the remote Pacific, but I was completely unaware that the local beasts didn't bite, the birds didn't fly away, and you could have a pleasant chat with an albatross as long as you spoke their language. This discovery is evidenced even before we put foot on shore, because when our zodiac boat pulls up to a tiny concrete dock on Espanola the sea lions don't bother to get out of the way. The concrete is warm and they simply lie there basking in the sun, none of them so much as batting an eye at the sight of knobby knees and hairy legs. Rafael warns us the mothers may get upset if we tread on their offspring, so best to give them a wide berth, and repeats the warning to never set foot off the path under punishment of being sent back to the ship.

I don't know if Charles Darwin chose Espanola as his first landing on the islands. Apparently his first discovery that led to his mindboggling and world changing work, usually referred to as the Theory of Evolution contained in his groundbreaking book *On the Origin of Species* published in 1859, came when he noticed the local finches using tools to build their nests. That is, they used twigs to move other twigs. The finches in Europe were either too stupid to use twigs, or didn't need to, or maybe there were no finches in Blighty, but small birds are not supposed to use tools. Evidently the ones who arrived in the Galapagos had been forced to innovate by circumstance. Adapt to this new strange environment or die. As boring as this may be to the average person, Darwin's subsequent discovery of the habits of the marine iguanas proved far more interesting.

One smells the iguanas before seeing them, and they are not hard to see. We tiptoe along the path, cameras in hand. Thousands of them, even tens of thousands of them, do exactly what iguanas are supposed to do, which is lie on the sand or rocks and bask in the sun. Iguanas are excellent baskers; they can do it for hours. Who more surprised than Darwin when he first spotted some of them crawling down to the ocean and slithering right in for a swim. Iguanas don't swim! It must have been like hearing a politician tell the truth for the first time. Darwin didn't have a camera but he closed his nose and made sharp note of the occasion. Then he sat down and started to study the local wildlife to find out what else was up. What he learned about the blue-footed boobies, frigate birds and marine iguanas and eventually published in his book had a profound effect on the world and continues to do so today.

Charles Darwin not only did not coin the phrase "survival of the fittest" (the phrase was invented by his colleague and philosopher Herbert Spencer), or its eventual evolvement into "dog-eat-dog," his work argued directly against the term. Darwin goes so far as to tie the success of human evolution (and even "lower animals") to the evolution of compassion. What Darwin wrote after his research in the Galapagos was the opposite

The sight of iguanas in the Galapagos swimming in the ocean to find food led to Charles Darwin's Theory of Evolution

of dog-eat-dog. "It is not the strongest of the species that survives," he wrote, "nor the most intelligent; it is the one most adaptable to change."

It was *The Principles of Biology* by Herbert Spencer (1864) that introduced the expression "survival of the fittest." According to the British Library, Spencer's work included writings on religion, economics, literature, biology, sociology, and political theory. He argued against the theories of Darwin and has been credited with the mistaken idea that "might is right," also known as "social Darwinism."

Darwin's book *On the Origin of Species* did not include human beings in its discussions of species evolution but his ideas were soon applied to human groups and organizations. The shorthand term "Darwinian" appeared very quickly after 1859 and by the late 1870s the phrase "social Darwinism" began to be heard and in the following decades was used to describe and justify a whole range of competing political and ideological positions.

The scale of social change during the 19th century because of industrialization, urbanization and technological innovation was unprecedented and led to Britain's competitive capitalist economy in which some people became enormously wealthy and others struggled amidst the direst poverty. Sound familiar? It was argued that markets should be allowed to operate freely, without government intervention, allowing wealth creation to flourish through competition. Social Darwinism confirmed this singular view: species compete and struggle and only some (the fittest and best) survive. Actually, Darwin wrote that cooperation was equally important, especially for those creatures, including humans, who live in groups.

Spencer argued that to try to help the weak flies in the face of nature. Attempts to aid the weakest in society, such as improving the living and working conditions of the poorest people, were dangerously mistaken and risked impeding the forces of "evolutionary advancement." Notions of competitiveness also often appeared in justifications of Britain's imperial ambitions. For instance, at the end of the 19th century there was fierce rivalry amongst European colonizers, keen to exploit mineral and other natural (i.e. "human") resources in Africa. Social Darwinists argued that Indigenous populations unable to withstand the greater military and economic power of a colonizing force must inevitably be pushed aside to make room for "fitter" competitors.

Similar ideas were important for Robert Knox, whose 1850 book *The Races of Man* classified and evaluated all human beings according to their race, and insisted that race was the most important determining feature of behavior and character. Arguments such as his were used to support the retention of slavery in the southern states of America. Darwin was horrified by slavery and his revolutionary ideas helped many Victorians to imagine a dynamic world of progress.

Towards the end of the 19th century, however, Darwin's theories of evolution became the basis of fears for social, racial and cultural degeneration and decline. Evolution was countered by frightening examples of "devolution," like Robert Louis Stevenson's book *Dr. Jekyll and Mr. Hyde* (1886), whose gentlemanly Jekyll turns into the beastly Hyde upon drinking a potion, whose squat, ape-like body, dark, hairy hands, and animal energy all signal a "primitive" state. The argument continues to this day and "survival of the fittest" is used as an excuse by many to exploit their fellow man. But I am reminded of another Darwin quote, perhaps less well known; "If the misery of the poor not be caused by the laws of nature, but by our institutions, great is our sin."

Strolling around the islands of Espanola, Floreana and Santa Cruz proves a real eye opener. I fall in love with the blue-footed boobies, who are so cute they hurt my feelings. One pair is attempting to build a nest right in the middle of the trail trod by ill-mannered tourists. I stop and watch. What I take to be the male of the species is hard at work dragging twigs, perhaps learned from the finches, and making a pile. He looks at me as if I am going to help or not. I know the rules and can't get involved. I take his portrait photo from a distance of about six inches, for which he is proud to pose, and feature it on the cover of my travel humor photobook *Amazing Adventures #1*.

The waved albatross, also known as Galapagos albatross, is the only member of the family Diomedeidae located in the tropics. When they forage, they follow a straight path to a single site off the coast of Peru, about 620 miles to the east. During the non-breeding season, these birds reside primarily on the Ecuadorian and Peruvian coasts, but they breed and raise their chicks on Espanola. I come around a corner and meet a chick sitting in the path sporting a huge grin and looking like it should have been an illustration by Sir John Tenniel in the original version of *Alice in Wonderland.* I sit and watch in wonder as those chicks old enough to fly waddle down a cliff and launch themselves into the air for the first time, to stay aloft for who knows how long. This island is the only place in the world a tourist can witness this magical event, and I feel privileged to watch.

Along with the rest of my group we get to watch a courtship ritual among the albatrosses, two males (as we are told by Rafael) and one female two-stepping around like a Cajun barn dance with free beer, snogging beaks together and chortling to themselves as only albatrosses can do. Wandering down the sandy beach I immediately become aware who is boss of the beach and it sure ain't me. There are sea lions everywhere, babies frolicking in the surf when not following me around, but when one investigates me to see if I have a proper tourist visa its mama follows, which means papa also has to stick his big nose into things, causing me to keep a sharp eye on him so he doesn't take a bite out of my bum.

Santa Cruz is the main island in the Galapagos, and in my innocence I expect to see a small cluster of wood or concrete block huts, a mistaken assumption and a clear indication that I should have done more homework. The Galapagos have become a prime tourist destination for those that can afford to travel that far, so the little fishing village has boomed, now sporting a population of 12,000 people. It has a hospital, restaurants, cafes with WiFi, banks, hotels, gift shops, and even night clubs. The main street is called Charles Darwin Avenida, and there is the Charles Darwin Foundation which is basically a zoo for tortoises and iguanas. Darwin is everywhere in the Galapagos.

At the top of the island is a small mountain where thousands of giant tortoises wander around at a responsible speed of about one mile per hour and are open to conversation if you ask nicely. I open up a chat with a younger and perhaps hipper member of the species, probably not even a hundred years old, but given the reputation of humans in the past for

Giant tortoises, formerly bred to use as foods on whaling ships, are the only creatures in the Galapagos that are afraid of humans.

making snacks and turtle soup out of his ancestors he soon retreats into his shell with a hiss, and I am left with only a photo and video of the occasion. Given the language differences it is hard to hold a philosophical conversation with a tortoise in the first place, so I never learn his opinion about Darwin's theories, but if you know how to live over 200 years then you have a right to think whatever you want.

Back down on the shore I wander along looking at the yachts in the marina, the marine iguanas swimming in the harbor, and the tourists pausing for selfies until I suddenly come across what I subsequently title "The Strangest Fish Shop in the World" in an article I publish in newspapers. Fish straight from the fishing boats is brought here, where two employees take turns whacking what looks like halibut into chunks. They have several assistants helping with packaging and deliveries. One is an immature sea lion who stands next to the butcher offering tips and suggestions, and for his or her work is rewarded with fish nibblies. There are two pelicans standing on the counter supervising carefully. This, I deduce, is a fish shop with a difference. If you can't afford a cruise around the islands with guided day tours, you can simply hang out at the Ayora fish store and learn that the wildlife in the Galapagos don't fear people, which is the way it should be in the rest of the world.

This charming scene makes me wonder about fishing in the Galapagos. How important is it? Before all the global tourists showed up to hold con-

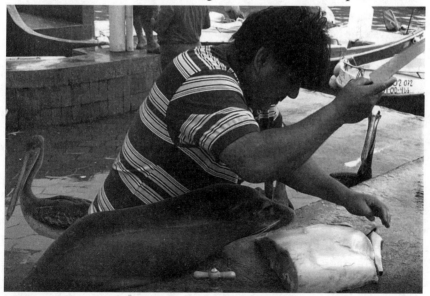

The fish shop on the island of Santa Cruz features sea lions and pelicans acting as supervisors.

79

versations with blue-footed boobies, fishing was the backbone of the local economy. What I discover to my horror is that foreign fishing fleets are strip-mining the local seas, and once again it is China that is doing most of the damage. According to a website called IUU (Illegal, Unreported and Unregulated) China is ranked as the world's worst nation for illegal fishing in the IUU fishing index. Its fleet, by far the largest in the world, is regularly implicated in overfishing, targeting of endangered shark species, illegal intrusion of jurisdiction, false licensing and catch documentation, and forced labor.

This massive and ongoing fishing effort of China's fleet threatens the Galápagos Islands, especially the rare fish species that only call the islands home and everyone that depends on it for food and livelihood. The Galápagos Marine Reserve is a UNESCO World Heritage Site and covers more than 133,000 square kilometers around the archipelago. It is an oasis for ocean biodiversity with more than 20 percent of its marine species found nowhere else on earth.

Five economies – mainland China, Taiwan, Japan, South Korea and Spain – account for 80 percent of the total catch from international waters. Coastal nations have introduced catch quotas and improved the monitoring and stewardship of fisheries in their Exclusive Economic Zones (EEZ), which extend 200 nautical miles from their shores. However, the waters beyond remain largely unregulated. The aggressiveness of the distant-water fishing (DWF) industry threatens the delicate balance of ecosystems across the world. Under China's "Going Out" strategy, adopted at the turn of the millennium to encourage the establishment and development of new overseas markets and supply lines for natural resources, fishing was identified as a strategic industry. Fuel subsidies were introduced and ever larger ships were built, and Chinese firms own over 2,900 DWF vessels, 40 percent of the world's total DWF fleet.

China is not a signatory to the Port State Measures Agreement (PSMA), the international framework for tackling illegal fishing, administered by the UN's Food and Agriculture Organization. The treaty obliges countries to verify ships' registrations and close their ports to those suspected of engaging in illegal activity, precluding the offload of illicit catch. According to the American Security Project, illegal, unreported, and unregulated (IUU) fishing violators are often engaged in global human trafficking trade and transnational organized crime. These crimes jeopardize international security on the high seas and are inherently hard to prosecute. After catch, the illegally sourced fish products make their way into the global market. As a result, unaware American consumers buy into this broken system, contributing to slavery at sea and transnational criminal activity.

For one example, an investigation by the Environmental Justice Foundation discovered extensive human rights violations committed against Ghanaian workers aboard Chinese-owned trawling vessels. Chinese vessel presence off the coast of West Africa is significant; one Chinese state enterprise operates 35 vessels in this region, with at least 17 located in Ghana alone. On these vessels, Ghanaian crew members were found to have been given unclean drinking water, denied food to maximize work productivity, physically assaulted by Chinese captains, and subjected to verbal threats. Ghanaian crew members slept above deck under a tarp, with limited opportunities to wash or bathe. All of the men interviewed claimed that they had not signed written contracts with their employers.

So, even here in the far reaches of the southern Pacific Ocean, as far away from the rest of the world as you can get, the malignant presence of the Chinese Communist Party rears its ugly head, strip-mining the oceans for profit at the risk of exterminating one of the world's most important food sources. The phrase "survival of the fittest" begins to take on a new meeaning, and I fly back to Ecuador musing that there is no escape from the clutches of the CCP, no matter where I travel.

FENTANYL

According to a Global TV report (Vancouver) the opioid crisis and record-setting death counts caused by fentanyl flooding into Canada are because of a growing diplomatic dispute with China. Canadian law enforcement agencies have found that fentanyl and its chemical precursors are mostly produced in southern China factories and sent to North America via shipping containers, and in the mail. Veterans in drug-trafficking investigations say that Canadian privacy and court procedure time limits also tend to severely limit pursuit of international criminals in Canada, in comparison to investigations by United States and Australian federal police. Canadian police must file hundreds of pages of evidence in order to get phone intercepts for suspected drug kingpins approved by judges. But in the U.S., they say, such processes require much less paperwork and a more practical standard of evidence. Australia and United States federal forces also have anti-drug trafficking policing operations in China that the RCMP lacks, sources said.

The kingpins of Canadian fentanyl have been linked by police to the Big Circle Boys, an organized crime group that traces its roots to China's

Cultural Revolution. During the 1960s, paramilitary groups known as Red Guards formed to purge those accused of being not sufficiently committed to China's communist revolution. The Red Guards were eventually themselves purged by the People's Liberation Army and sent to the city of Guangzhou (formerly Canton) for "re-education." Upon their escape or release, some formed criminal organizations known for their violence, notably in Hong Kong. The name Big Circle Boys, or Dai Huen Jai, came from Chinese maps that de-marked Guangzhou with a large circle.

In the 1980s, Big Circle members began migrating, some to Vancouver. By the 1990s they were all across Canada. "The BCB do business in small independent groups or cells, unlike the highly-organized structure of Triads," according to a report prepared for the B.C. government. Long before fentanyl, the Big Circle Boys were involved in drug trafficking and credit card fraud. Big Circle also made what a Canadian judge called "enormous profits" trafficking heroin. The Big Circle Boys have cooperated with other underworld organizations, including Hong Kong triads, the Hells Angels and the Italian mafia. But they differ in that they are "a loosely affiliated group of gangs rather than a single, centrally-led organization," according to a *Jane's Intelligence Review* report. Thanks to the CCP turning a blind eye to fentanyl factories in China, a huge number of Canadians die every year

CHAPTER EIGHT

FINDING THE MEANING
OF LIFE IN JAMAICA

Greed is not a financial issue. It's a heart issue.
- Andy Stanley

hat is the meaning of life? Wikipedia may be the worst possible place to look for answers, but if you google that question their reply comes at the top of the page so a lot of people must look to Wikipedia for answers. Their definition, as always, is opaque and doesn't really provide any clear answers. *"The meaning of life, as we perceive it, is derived from philosophical and religious contemplation of, and scientific inquiries about existence, social ties, consciousness, and happiness. Many other issues are also involved, such as symbolic meaning, ontology, value, purpose, ethics, good and evil, free will, the existence of one or multiple gods, conceptions of God, the soul, and the afterlife."* Does that help clear the picture? No?

Googling many other articles and definitions results in one common denominator, which is "having a meaningful existence." I think there is a great deal of truth in that statement. After all, if your life is pointless, what's the point? Just throw a stick for dogs to fetch and see how happy they become. Fetching the stick serves a purpose; for many dogs it is ingrained in their genetic makeup, although I don't know the value of shih tzu lap dogs. People are much the same, although I suggest throwing a stick for many to fetch won't do the trick. In fact, if you ask most people about the meaning of life they will look at you as if you are shih tzu.

I think the best place to find the meaning of life is at a school, which is why I went to the elementary school in Ocho Rios in Jamaica. I had wangled a free trip to Jamaica simply by contacting Sandals Resorts and explaining to them that the hottest new travel trend is "meaningful travel," and they should get in on the action. I suspect the most popular and profitable travel trend in North America remains flying to Cancun and getting drunk on the beach, but since I have no interest in that sort of experience I refrained from mentioning it.

Why, I said to the Sandals PR department, I would be so kind as to stay at their resort (for free) and subject myself to a week of exploration of the "meaningful trips" that were possible in the vicinity of their resort, skipping the usual beach life and golf, and write a story for Canadian newspapers whose readers are so desperate for a sunshine story in the middle of winter they will tolerate a travel story "with meaning," as long as there is a photo of a place that looks warm. Actually, I stole the story idea after coming across an organization called "Pack for a Purpose," which suggests that bringing appropriate gifts like school supplies to "developing countries" makes both the giver and receiver happy. The PR department had done their homework and agreed to my theory, so Bob's your uncle and I snagged a free trip to Jamaica.

Actually, you would have to read the Sandals Ocho Rios website with a microscope to find out about any available "meaningful trips." I discovered the opportunity by reading Pack for a Purpose. Sandals have many different resorts in the Caribbean, especially Jamaica, and the Ocho Rios resort was targeted mostly towards honeymooners. Quite frankly, I found it was a kissy face destination but no matter. If you asked nicely, as I did, you will discover that Sandals has a small team dedicated towards serving customers who want to do more than lie on the beach and smooch in the elevators. The team even has a van and will take you to various non-tourist places for free! The PFAP website suggested that the school supplies would be most appreciated, or even a donation, but I already knew all that, having donated many different gifts in countries ranging from Nepal to the Dominican Republic, while carefully considering any negative aftereffects.

Our first stop is with Mel Tenant, a retired British teacher who has a house near Oracabessa beach not far from Ocho Rios. Mel discovered several years ago that the beach is home for hawksbill sea turtles, a species threatened with extinction. They lay their eggs in the sand, the eggs hatch baby turtles that swim out to sea and paddle around for 5 years and come back to the exact spot to lay their own eggs. There is a serious problem in that local birds like to eat the baby turtles as the tiny creatures make a dash to the sea. Volunteers, like the guests from Sandals, are encouraged to drop by and help save the baby turtles by washing them clean at birth, and watching over them as they make a dash to the ocean, thereby setting their radar for life.

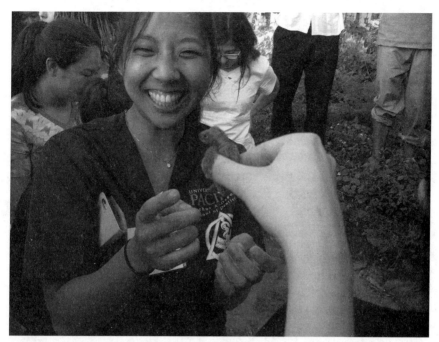

A dental student from the U.S. is part of a group thrilled to assist with the birth of baby turtles.

Today there is a large crowd, dozens of American dental students who have volunteered to come to Ocho Rios to provide free dental care to the poor people of that town. The young students delight in the delivery of the baby turtles that emerge out of the sand the size of potato chips. I am handed my own baby turtle, perhaps 30 seconds old, who looks at me with its big brown eyes and says: "What the heck is going on?" I name him or her Usain, after the Jamaican sprinter, wash its shell and watch as Usain makes a mighty and successful sprint to the sea along with 182 other baby sea turtles, all to the chagrin of the seagulls that hover in the sky above and scream in anger.

The next day I ask to attend the dental clinic held in the town. I will be the first to admit that dental clinics are not a prime tourist attraction, but I want to interview the students about their reasons for volunteering. "It makes me happy to do this," is their common refrain. It makes me happy to know that such good work is being done in the world, and then we are off to the local primary school where I get to meet with the little kids and act like Santa Claus, bringing them magic markers and coloring books (one for the girls, one for the boys, which I give to the teacher) in which they can draw if they do their homework. I am swarmed with hugs and kisses and it is honestly one of the warmest feelings I have ever experienced on my journeys around the world.

Next up is a middle school, where a group of young girls is busy in the computer lab learning how to keyboard and google. The principal explains that the computers are gifts from Sandals, from money donated by the resort's guests. I explain to the principal that I have a quest; I want to ask the girls an important question and shoot video of the experience to share with my own readers and viewers. I want to ask the girls to research the definition of the meaning of life, using a computer. The principal breaks out laughing. "Michael, these girls are only 8 years old!"

Nonetheless I persevere. "Girls, can you type? Do you know how to ask Mr. Google-in-the-box questions? Do you know how to save the reply?" They do know how, and they excitedly type in the question. In a matter of seconds comes the reply. "The meaning of life is to be happy." They burst out laughing, as does the teacher and I sport a big grin myself. They are learning how to spell, how to do math, how to type and write, but I think they have learned a valuable lesson today, as will perhaps the people who watch my videos about "transformative travel, how to change the world on your journey through life."

Should you ask a student in North America the same question about the meaning of life, I suggest you might find a different reply. From listening to their parents or teachers, or absorbing lessons from social and mainstream media, I suggest the reply might be "to become a success,"

Thanks to Mr. Google schoolgirls in Jamaica discover the meaning of life is to "be happy."

which implies making money and gaining fame. You need a lot of money to be a success in North America these days. Failure, on the other hand, is free. Nothing could be a bigger success than to become a "celebrity," whether a singer or an athlete or someone in the public eye who makes a fortune. It doesn't matter how you do it because – as the social Darwinists will tell you - the end justifies the means. On the far right of the political arena, "not getting caught and going to prison" is the same as "doing the right thing" used to be at one time for them. Leaders in modern society, whether politicians or business people, lie and cheat and steal and become rich and famous in the process. Making money is their chief goal, as if money automatically brings happiness. Saving sea turtles or supporting dental clinics is not a part of the process. My bet is that the young school girls in Ocho Rios know better.

BLACK GOLD

So, where did the money come from in the first place to launch the Chinese Economic Miracle? The word is that Prescott Bush Jr. travelled to Shenzhen and started handing it out. It's doubtful it came from Prescott's own pocket or from the sleazy Bush Family fortune made from building munitions factories for Hitler and the Nazi Party in the 1930s. Once again we turn to our friends at Wikipedia, never a perfect source but always a good place to start looking.

For several decades before World War Two, the Japanese had been looting and pillaging, stealing whatever they could find all over Southeast Asia, to fund their upcoming war effort. According to various sources that Wikipedia does not name, the loot was initially stashed in Singapore and later transported to the Philippines. The stolen property reportedly included many different kinds of valuables looted from banks, depositories, other commercial premises, museums, private homes, and religious buildings. It became known as Yamashita's Gold, getting its name from General Tomoyuki Yamashita, who assumed command of the Japanese forces in the Philippines in 1944. The plan was to ship the treasure from the Philippines to the Japanese Home Islands after the war ended. However, as the War in the Pacific progressed, the Japanese got their asses kicked by the Yanquis.

Investigative journalist Sterling Seagrave and his wife Peggy wrote two books related to the subject: *The Yamato Dynasty: The Secret History of Japan's Imperial Family* (2000) and *Gold Warriors: America's Secret Recovery of Yamashita's Gold* (2003). The Seagraves contend that looting, including more than 6,000 tons of gold, was organized on a massive scale by Yakuza gangsters such as Yoshio Kodama and the highest levels of Japanese society, including Emperor Hirohito. The Seagraves allege that Hirohito appointed his brother, Prince Yasuhito Chichibu, to create a secret organization named Kin No Yuri or "Golden Lily," to hide the gold. Many of those who knew the locations of the loot were killed during the war, or later tried by the Allies for war crimes and executed. Yamashita himself was convicted of war crimes and executed by the United States Army on February 23, 1946, in the Philippines.

According to the Seagraves, numerous Golden Lily vaults were found by Edward Lansdale and Santa Romana in caves north of Manila. They allege that Romana tortured Yamashita's driver Major Kojima Kashii to obtain the probable locations of the loot. Romana was a Filipino-American commando who fought in the Philippines during World War II and had witnessed Japanese placing very heavy boxes in tunnels and caves. Also, United States Navy Warrant Officer John Ballinger, disguised as a fisherman, had witnessed Japanese offloading very heavy boxes full of gold from a hospital ship in early 1945.

The Seagraves wrote that Lansdale flew to Tokyo and briefed General Douglas MacArthur and his Chief of Intelligence officer, who later flew to the United States to brief Clark Clifford, a top advisor to President Harry Truman. They returned to inspect several caves in Philippines with MacArthur. More than 170 tunnels and caves were found. The Seagraves allege 176 "black gold" banking accounts were subsequently created in 42 countries after moving the loot by ship to support future United States "black ops." And President Nixon "gave" some of the gold back to Mao.

Wikipedia ends its history of Yamashita's Gold stating that with a total worth of over $50 trillion in 2009, one Black Eagle Trust numbered account deposited with HSBC was a certificate of time deposit worth $93 billion on September 15, 2004. In his 1999 book *The CIA's Black Ops: Covert Action, Foreign Policy, and Democracy*, author John Jacob Nutter states that since 1947 the Central Intelligence Agency has secretly worked to subvert foreign powers and even overthrow enemy governments to further United States influence abroad. The vast array of CIA "black ops" including covert acts against Saddam Hussein, international terrorists, secret Afghan missions, the overthrow of Guatemalan leaders, assassination plots against Castro and others, domestic and foreign narcotics conspiracies, underground Mafia relations, and even controversial plans to dupe top U.S. officials has stretched the CIAs influence far beyond its original purpose. It has in fact become an underground Department of Foreign Affairs.

A member of the Association of Former Intelligence Officers, Dr. Nutter reveals that the U.S. has become enamored with covert action; that black ops have become U.S. foreign policy; and that the CIA has developed into a policy maker, dangerously independent of the government that created it. Nutter explains the many and varied types of covert CIA action like subsidies, graymail, propaganda, psychological and economic warfare, military support, paramilitary operations, coups d'etat, and assassinations. He provides detailed examples of success and failure undertaken in the name of "national security."

The peace and quiet of Jamaica notwithstanding, the world continues to become a more dangerous place every day. However, the revival of the sea turtles is a sign that disasters and extinction can be halted if good people come to the front of the fray and get involved. Just don't ask the CIA to participate.

The Shard, pictured from Great Tower Street at St. Mary at Hill.
Creative Commons EE Paul

CHAPTER NINE

THE LATEST BLITZ OF LONDON

We cannot negotiate with people who say what's mine is mine and what's yours is negotiable.

– John F. Kennedy

F inding a Chinese presence in London, England is a challenging task. I thought Toronto was the most multi-cultural city in the world until I arrived in London. Strolling down the streets there appears to be a face from every race in the world, which I am told was a factor in England's irrational decision to pull out of the European Union via Brexit. "Too many foreigners," brayed the elderly pensioners, sipping on their tea and nibbling on scones while turning up their noses. Indeed, there are Indians, Muslims, Africans and even pink people, but the Chinese are not much in attendance, visually, although beneath the surface they are making their mark, in real estate as always.

We start our strolling just south of the Thames River, where a grotesque monstrosity named The Shard has been erected, a glass and steel skyscraper like those found in most cities, this one looking rather unfinished due to its jagged rooftop. My wife is on a mission to visit every museum in the world, and since half of them are in London she is in heaven. I follow dutifully with an eye more on the architecture than on museums. We visit the Tate, the London Museum, the Royal Whatever and the Sir John Soames house turned Museum, easily my favorite because you half expect Dumbledore or Harry Potter to appear out of the cobwebs. Sir John was an architect, collector and certified nutbar as his collection of bric a brac, paintings, sculpture, architectural fragments, models, books, drawings and furniture prove. I didn't find out if he actually purchased his pieces or merely borrowed them as was the British colonial habit at the time. All the major museums in London seem to exhibit ancient artifacts casually taken from Greece, Italy and the Middle East and not returned, yet.

Chinese investment in London commercial property has more than trebled since Britain voted to leave the EU, most of the loot channeled through Hong Kong at a time of heightened political uncertainty in the former British colony. Investors largely from Hong Kong are snapping up the British capital's best-known skyscrapers, including the "Cheesegrater" and the "Walkie Talkie." Recently Chinese investors spent £3.96 billion on London commercial property, according to data from the CBRE real estate group, the highest amount on record and outpacing the £2.69 billion spent in the previous year. Hong Kong accounted for 92 percent of the Chinese investment, according to the Knight Frank agency.

Hong Kong food conglomerate Lee Kum Kee paid £1.28 billion for 20 Fenchurch Street, the 34-storey skyscraper known as the Walkie Talkie, a record for an office building in Britain. With Beijing cracking down on foreign deals by mainland companies, investors there are using Hong Kong as a conduit for overseas deals.

Several factors are drawing the huge level of investment, including sterling's 12 percent drop against the U.S. dollar since the Brexit referendum – to which the Hong Kong dollar is pegged. The Brexit vote means some London-based financial jobs will shift to the continent or Ireland, so that banks can continue selling to clients in the EU. But this negative factor for the office market is offset by the pound's fall, which makes property cheaper for foreign investors. Capital from China and Hong Kong has accounted for a third of all investment in London commercial real estate recently, up from less than 10 percent before the referendum, according to CBRE (Coldwell Banker Richard Ellis).

There is a full police contingent standing guard outside #10 Downing Street; we find the Harrod's food court boasts the world's most expensive seafood; Big Ben and the Parliament buildings are gorgeous architecture;

and we enjoy a subway ride up to Camden Town, where the food stalls are the complete opposite to Harrods, selling every type of cheap cuisine you could imagine from Ethiopian to Indian, but not a fish and chips stand in the bunch.

According to the Hurun Chinese Luxury Consumer Survey 2020, Chinese high-net-worth individuals have placed 12.5 percent of their wealth into overseas assets, with London ranked as the most popular investment destination. In 2019, Office for National Statistics data showed that buyers from the Chinese mainland and Hong Kong invested 7.69 billion pounds ($10.6 billion) in London property, including more than 750 million pounds in residential property in the City of Westminster and the Royal Borough of Kensington and Chelsea. Realtors are confident that London's position as a global financial powerhouse remains unchanged, as does its standing as a go-to location for education and as a safe haven for overseas investors.

According to the *Guardian* newspaper, over the past decade Chinese investment worth more than £50 billion has flowed into Britain's economy. From the telecoms networks to London's famous black cabs, football clubs and Pizza Express, the Chinese yuan can be felt infiltrating Britain's economy and its national infrastructure. Chinese steelmaker Jingye completed a £1.2 billion deal to save British Steel earlier, saving 3,000 jobs. It is not China's first multibillion-pound move into British industry. The Bank of China was among the lenders that came to the rescue of carmaker Jaguar Land Rover with £560 million of loans after it struggled to get help from the British government. Aluminium Corporation of China, better known as Chinalco, also owns almost 15 percent of Anglo-Australian miner Rio Tinto, and the Chinese state's sovereign wealth fund, China Investment Corporation (CIC), snapped up a stake in Britain's largest water supplier, Thames Water, as part of a consortium of investors and foreign funds.

CIC's interests extend beyond water to gas supply, too. It became one of the owners of Britain's gas pipeline system after joining a consortium of investors that acquired the business from National Grid in 2016. It is one of many Chinese investors at the heart of the U.K.'s energy system. China National Offshore Oil Corporation (CNOOC) has for years been responsible for around a quarter of the U.K. North Sea's oil production, including output from the biggest remaining oilfield. Meanwhile CGN, China's state nuclear company, is eyeing Britain's energy future. It has an almost one-third stake in plans to build the U.K.'s first new nuclear power plant in a generation. Eventually, CGN hopes to build its own nuclear plant at Bradwell, Essex, a prospect that has caused alarm within Britain's energy industry.

The Chinese state fund's influence extends to Britain's main international transport hub at Heathrow, too, after it paid £450 million to buy a 10 percent stake in the airport in 2012. The black cabs queueing for fares at Heathrow's pick-up points are built with Chinese investment too; Geely, an automotive company based in Hangzhou, owns the company that builds the LEVC hybrid black cabs in Coventry.

We take the subway back downtown from Camden Town and amble across the Millennium Bridge back over the Thames. We pause to people watch and look at the famous skyline. From this perspective London looks almost medieval, aside from several ugly modern high rise buildings stabbing into the sky, but hidden behind that false front is the understanding that China is buying up Britain, and nobody seems to notice.

The new Millennium Bridge spans the ancient River Thames in downtown London.

THE POWELL MANIFESTO

In June 2022 the United States took a sharp turn backwards, legally and morally. In one disastrous week the Supreme Court ruled that it was perfectly legal for Americans to carry a concealed weapon. Hey, why not, the world is full of bad guys and you never know when there is going to be a gunfight! This ruling came despite the fact that earlier in the week yet more school children were gunned down in their classrooms in Texas, the latest in a long string of similar mass murders in American schools, churches and shopping malls. Worse yet, a few days later the Court attacked women's rights that had taken decades to achieve, ruling that Roe versus Wade would be overturned. Justice Clarence Thomas hinted darkly that similar "liberal" decisions made by earlier Courts would also be overturned in the future, causing great consternation in the LGBT+, Black, and other minority communities. Headlines around the world reverberated in shock. What the hell was going on? Has America gone completely insane?

Comments flew back and forth in both social and mainstream media. How did this happen? When did the Far Right start its dirty work to turn back the clock on social change and return America to being a white, male dominated, Christian theocracy like the Good Old Days when women's place was in the kitchen and Blacks were lucky to ride at the back of the bus? I read all the articles and opinions and tweets I could absorb, finally stumbling across a tweet by retired Vancouver radio talk show host Jon McComb. "You have to read this," he tweeted, regarding the history of the Supreme Court. So I followed the string of tweets and re-tweets.

There were numerous tweets in regards to exactly what the Far Right was up to, with some tweets walking the story back to specific events that had already happened to act as precursors to the new Supreme Court ruling. Several made reference to a document titled the Powell Manifesto, claiming "this is where the BS all started." Never having heard about this document, I made a note to google the topic and learn more. Wouldn't you know it, the trail leads back again to Tricky Dick in 1971.

According to Wikipedia (never the best source, but if you simply want basic history it's OK) Lewis Franklin Powell Jr. (September 19, 1907 - August 25, 1998) was an American lawyer and jurist who served on the Supreme Court of the United States from 1971 to 1987. He first worked for Hunton & Williams, a large law firm in Richmond, Virginia, focusing on corporate law, especially representing wealthy clients such as the Tobacco Institute. Hey, if you want to get rich, fight the fight against stopping lung cancer! In 1971, President Richard Nixon appointed Powell to succeed Justice Hugo Black on the Court. Powell finally retired from the Court during the administration of President Ronald Reagan, and was eventually succeeded by Anthony Kennedy.

Powell was actually known as something of a liberal at the time, given how conservative America was in 1971. He was among the 7-2 majority on the Court who legalized abortion in the United States in Roe v.

Wade (1973). Powell's pro-choice stance on abortion stemmed from an incident during his tenure at his law firm, when the girlfriend of one of Powell's office staff bled to death from an illegal self-induced abortion. Powell sat on the boards of 11 major corporations, including the tobacco giant Philip Morris, and reportedly amassed a personal fortune fighting against efforts to curtail the use of tobacco. Powell fought hard against any restrictions on smoking by arguing that research had not yet proven tobacco caused cancer, and hey! People had the right to smoke, even if dying from lung cancer hurts a bit!

Powell has been widely commemorated as a "centrist," a lifelong Democrat and a judicial workhorse, writing more than 500 legal opinions, but his most significant contribution to American legal history was made in secret, some five months before his elevation to the bench, and it was anything but moderate. On August 23, 1971, Powell penned a confidential 6,400-word memorandum and sent it off to a friend, Eugene Sydnor Jr., then chairman of the U.S. Chamber of Commerce Education Committee. The memo, titled "Attack on American Free Enterprise System," was breathtaking in its scope and ambition, and far more right-wing than anything ever published by any Supreme Court judge. It was later referred to by critics as "A Call to Arms for Class War."

"No thoughtful person can question that the American economic system is under broad attack," Powell began his analysis. "There always have been some who opposed the American system, and preferred socialism or some form of statism (communism or fascism). But now what concerns us," he continued, "is quite new in the history of America. We are not dealing with sporadic or isolated attacks from a relatively few extremists or even from the minority socialist cadre. Rather, the assault on the enterprise system is broadly based and consistently pursued. It is gaining momentum and converts."

"Strength," Powell wrote, "lies in organization, in careful long-range planning and implementation, in consistency of action over an indefinite period of years, in the scale of financing available only through joint effort, and the political power available only through united action and national organizations." Deepening his call to action, Powell urged the Chamber of Commerce and other business entities to redouble their lobbying efforts and to recruit lawyers of the greatest skill to represent business interests before the Supreme Court. "Under our constitutional system, the judiciary may be the most important instrument for social, economic and political change."

The conservative right, starting with seed money from the Coors Brewing family and Richard Mellon Scaife's publishing empire, moved forward to implement virtually every element of the Powell memo. It is a story of how the Far Right – in spite of political differences, ego, and competing priorities – were able to cooperate and to develop a methodology that drives their issues and values relentlessly to this day.

Lewis Franklin Powell, Jr., Associate Justice of the Supreme Court of the United States (1972–1987)

Starting with just a handful of groups, including the Heritage Foundation in the early '70s, the conservatives built a new generation of organizations – think tanks, media monitors, legal groups, networking organizations, all driven by the same over-arching values of free enterprise, individual freedom and limited government. Then there is the "investment banking matrix," about 200 key people who personally invest hundreds of thousands of dollars a year; 135 of them also serve on the boards of the "Big 80" groups.

Then there is also the conservative media machine, which operated at full power to get George W. Bush and Donald Trump elected. Conservatives and their allies were able to magnify their message through a network of right-leaning TV and radio channels, including Rupert Murdoch's Fox News Channel, which provides the Far Right with a 24/7 campaign infomercial – for free. Here was a news network with more viewers than CNN and MSNBC combined, constantly repeating, often verbatim, the messages out of the White House under any Far Right administration.

More help comes from religious broadcasters. "Under the radar screen, the Christian Church community has created a formidable electronic media infrastructure and now plays a major role influencing public opinion," wrote Jeffrey Chester, Executive Director of the Center for Digital Democracy (CDD). "The religious media are producing and distributing 'news,' commentary and cultural guides, and their reach and influence are undeniable."

The Far Right's electoral victories have proved that the conservatives have achieved dominance over the flow of information to the American people, says the CDD, so much so that even a well-run Democratic campaign stands virtually no chance for national success without major changes in the media system. The Republican victories highlight perhaps the greatest failure of the Democratic/liberal side in American politics: a refusal to invest in the development of a comparable system for distributing information that can counter the Far Right's potent media infrastructure. Democrats and liberals have refused to learn from the lessons of the Republican/conservative success.

Let's give the last word to Noam Chomsky, the well-known leftish speaker and activist for democracy, speaking about the Powell manifesto in 2017:

> Powell didn't actually say that business is losing control. What he said is it's being beaten down by the massive forces of the left, which have taken over everything. He says they've taken over the media, they've taken over the universities, they're practically in control of the whole country. And meanwhile, the poor, embattled business community can barely survive under this incredible assault. It's a very interesting picture.
>
> You should pay attention to the rhetoric. It's kind of like a spoiled 3-year-old who expects to have everything, and somebody takes a piece of candy away from him, and they have a tantrum. The world's ending! That's pretty much the picture. Of course, business was essentially running everything, but not totally. There were some democratizing tendencies in the '60s. The public became more engaged in public affairs and was considered a serious threat. So he calls on the business community to defend itself from this monstrous attack. Look, after all, we're the ones who have the resources. We have the funds. You know, we're the trustees of the universities. We should be able to protect ourselves from this assault that's wiping out the American way, business and so on.
>
> The Powell Memorandum is literally a tantrum. It's saying that democracy is simply a threat. The population has to be restored to passivity, then everything will be fine. The quite remarkable fact is that mortality is increasing among middle-class, lower-middle-class, working-class white Americans, middle-aged white Americans. That's something unknown in developed societies. Mortality keeps declining there. Here it's increasing. And the roots of it are what are called diseases of despair. People don't have hope

for the future, and for pretty good reasons if you look at the facts of the matter. Real male wages today are pretty much at the level of the '60s.'

Right at the peak of euphoria, right before the 2008 crash, real wages for American workers were lower than they were in 1979, when the "neo-liberal experiments" were just beginning. These affect people's lives seriously. They're not starving. These are not the poorest people. You know, they're kind of surviving, but without a sense of dignity, of worth, of hope for the future, of some meaning in your life, and so on. So they're reacting in often very self-destructive ways."

According to the Far Right, the shootings in schools and churches would diminish if there were simply more police and more guns. Arm the teachers! Teach the kids to fight back! So the Supreme Court in 2022 turns back the clock to 1971, when Tricky Dick was still in the White House planning burglaries, and appointing judges like Lewis Powell to sit on the Court and turn back the clock to a time when women and Blacks did what they were told. If Powell was still alive, no doubt he would take great pleasure in witnessing the damage his Manifesto started, simply through a note he sent to the Chamber of Commerce.

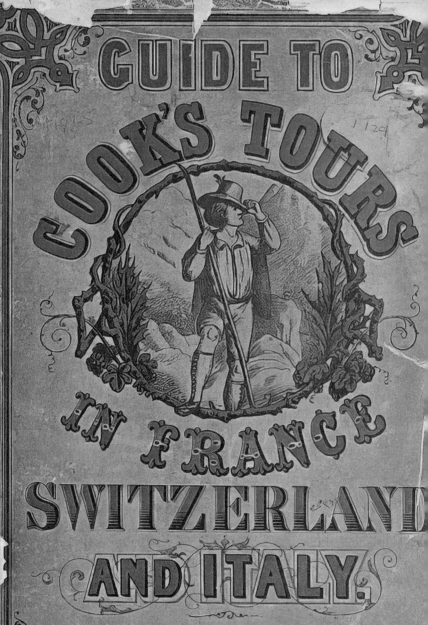

GUIDE TO
COOK'S TOURS
IN FRANCE
SWITZERLAND
AND ITALY.

COMPILED AND PUBLISHED BY
THO.S COOK TOURIST MANAGER

TOURIST OFFICE 98 FLEET STREET, LONDON
AND 63 GRANBY STREET, LEICESTER

SOLD BY TWEEDIE 337 STRAND LONDON
AT THE CHIEF BOOKSTANDS OF
W. H. SMITH & SON.

AND BY ALL BOOKSELLERS

Chapter 10

The Grand Tour of Switzerland

Ayn Rand's "philosophy" is nearly perfect in its immorality, which makes the size of her audience all the more ominous and symptomatic as we enter a curious new phase in our society.... To justify and extol human greed and egotism is to my mind not only immoral, but evil.

— Gore Vidal

On August 4th 1845, in the midst of the Industrial Revolution, a British entrepreneur named Thomas Cook arranged accommodations for a party of rich folks to travel by rail from Leicester to Liverpool. It was a success. Following that, in 1847 Cook launched "grand tours of Europe" for the newly rich British industrialists to travel to Switzerland and enjoy the unpolluted air in the mountains. Such were the humble beginnings of what has since become known as "the tourism industry," now one of the world's largest businesses. That same Grand Tour of Switzerland 150 years ago is still available for selection for those travelers who know where to go.

The kind folks at Swiss Tourism, using Search Engine Optimization, noticed my byline appearing in many newspaper articles all across Canada. I was invited to watch a webinar on my computer about their country, and subsequently invited to invent a story line that would interest as many Canadian newspaper readers as possible. I decide that re-creating a Thomas Cook Grand Tour would be the way to go. History! Swiss tradition! The kind folks at Swiss Tourism agree, and to pay the freight.

Whereas Cook's tours went slowly by boat and carriage, today the modern traveler flies directly to Zurich, a global banking centre. Centred around the Limmat River, the town reflects the old Grand Tour glory with its cobblestone streets, tall church spires and bustling cafes along the river. I am invited to take my accommodation at the glorious Widder Hotel, originally built in the 12th century as a warehouse. Today the Widder is the epitome of classic Swiss service and charm, its original stone walls of 1192 standing in sharp contrast with the hotel's modern plasma TVs and see-through glass elevators.

I have a secret card that I do not divulge to my hosts. Also Named Michael lives now in Zurich and I am invited to stay with him for a week before beginning my Grand Tour. We explore the city and I learn its history. For instance, Bahnhofstrasse is Zürich's main downtown street and one of the world's most expensive and exclusive shopping avenues. In 2011, a study named the Bahnhofstrasse the most expensive street for retail property in all of Europe and perhaps the world. Over the years the street has managed to attract the crème de la crème of the world's business community, its most famous jewelers, watch and clock firms, hoteliers and bankers, and the clamor for space on the street has been so insistent that the price of land had soared to double that of Fifth Avenue rate in New York.

According to an exposé by PBS TV, Switzerland's reputation as a "neutral safe-haven" during World War II revealed the entire gamut of Swiss financial dealings with the Nazis. Swiss banks have long been a favored repository of capital from unstable countries. Before the Second World War, with the rise of Nazism many Jews in Central and East Europe sought to protect their assets by depositing money in Swiss accounts, and their valuables in Swiss safe deposit boxes. To encourage such transfers, in 1934 the Swiss even strengthened special banking secrecy laws which facilitated preservation of the anonymity of depositors.

Switzerland also served as a repository for vast quantities of gold and other valuables plundered by the Nazis from Jews all over Europe. Right up until the end of the war, Switzerland laundered hundreds of millions of dollars in stolen assets, including gold taken from the central banks of German-occupied Europe. At the war's end Switzerland successfully resisted Allied calls to restitute these funds, and in the Washington Agreement of 1946 the Allies received only 12 percent of the stolen gold. Holocaust survivors and the heirs of those who perished met a wall of bureaucracy and only a handful managed to reclaim their assets. Swiss banks had also done a lucrative business with the German Reichsbank and with individual Nazi officials. Symbolically, even the royalties from Hitler's *Mein Kampf* were deposited in a Swiss bank account.

Toward the end of the war, when other neutral states refused to purchase gold directly from Germany, Switzerland continued to carry on this highly profitable trade. That gold generally came from two sources; the gold reserves of the central banks of the occupied countries and gold stolen from individuals. Documents uncovered in former East German archives suggest that in 1944 SS Chief and German Interior Minister Heinrich Himmler sent a special train loaded with hundreds of millions

Switzerland is a country awash both in history and other people's carefully stored money.

of dollars of gold, jewelry and art objects to Switzerland for deposit in the vaults of Swiss banks. Diamonds stolen from over 1,000 firms in German-occupied Belgium were sold to Swiss dealers. Swiss art dealers trafficked in art seized from Jews and others. The rumor is that much of the plunder still lies hidden in the vaults underneath the street. Certainly Switzerland is one of the world's richest countries.

I wander down the street thoughtfully, peering in windows at the world's most expensive watches. I am reminded of my attempt to write a story about Rodeo Drive in Beverly Hills where I planned to smuggle my camera into the stores and take photos of steely-eyed elderly ladies buying $10,000 jewel-encrusted bedroom slippers to add to their collection, but I never made it past the doormen. Here in Zurich I make no attempt to get past the doormen, sharp-eyed and well-dressed young fellows who eyeball the prospective customers and decide who to let inside the premises. What interests me more are the customers; male and female, young and old, most of them are Chinese. It's a long way from Beijing, I think, and a strange place to find Chinese tourists, but what do I know?

From Zurich, today's tourist can jump aboard the many punctual, clean and high-speed Swiss trains and whisk oneself right across the country in a matter of hours. An hour east of Zurich by rail, travelers have been flocking to the resort of Bad Ragaz since the "healing waters" were discovered in 1242 by hunters in a nearby gorge. Eventually the waters were diverted into a tunnel and these days are piped directly to the Grand Resort, the ultimate definition of what a luxury spa should be. Resort guests can enjoy a vast variety of spa and medical services, including laser and plastic surgery, from a team of up to 70 doctors. While I enjoy my stay, I am amazed by the high number of Chinese tourists.

While the traveler could spend weeks wallowing at Bad Ragaz if the wallet allowed, this would mean missing out on Lake Country, centred around the extremely pleasant town of Lucerne, where the Palace Hotel became one place for Cook's clients to spend entire summers. Paddle wheelers still take passengers on tours of Lake Lucerne, stopping at many agreeable little villages and hotels. At the far eastern end, the traveler resumes the Grand Tour via the William Tell Express train. Fresh air and high mountains initially inspired the German writer Goethe to wax poetic about the health and beauty of the Swiss Alps. Britain during the Industrial Revolution was as heavily polluted as today's China, so Thomas Cook promoted fresh air as the reason for a Swiss mountain vacation. But the Chinese tourist of today shows little interest in hiking in the mountains. They are found standing in long lines outside the jewelry stores of downtown Lucerne.

"Why are these people so fascinated with jewelry?" I ask a security guard standing outside a shop in the pouring rain. "Do they like to play dress-up and go for fancy dinners?"

"No, the jewelry is for re-sale," he replies, looking at me as if I am stupid. "They buy it here and sell it for more to richer people back in Shanghai. It is a big business."

"You mean there are even richer people than these tourists who can afford to fly to Switzerland and buy $10,000 watches?"

"Of course," he says, looking down his nose at me. "A $10,000 watch is nothing to the Chinese billionaires. There is always a line-up around the block here."

I am invited to dinner with the general manager of the very grand Palace Hotel where I am staying courtesy of the Tourism Board. It is indeed a palace. She is a gracious and well-spoken young lady with great manners and orders the speciality of the house for me, a whole lake fish baked in salt in an oven. Swiss food is not my favorite; this meal tastes like a fish cooked in salt. While we are eating there is a commotion in the lobby to which she must attend, some sort of shouting. I quietly follow to see what the fuss is about. It is a Chinese bus tour, some of the passengers appear to be drunk, and some are yelling while spitting on the floor in anger at the wait for check-in.

I slink back to our table and the manager soon returns as well, red-faced and embarrassed. The Palace has long been an attraction for the rich, royalty and celebrities. The clientele is changing, she admits, with Chinese bus tours and other guests of that ilk now comprising most of the business. They have not been taught good manners, she says. In fact, she admits with tears in her eyes that the hotel has just been sold to a Chinese billionaire. I finish my rock-encrusted lake fish and wish I had requested a fondue instead. I am fond of cheese, and Swiss cheese comes from contented cows, although I fear that contentment may soon be changing as well.

RAND CORPORATION SURVEY EXPLAINS THE ECONOMIC IMBALANCE IN THE U.S.

A September 2020 feature article in the magazine *Fast Company* helps to explain the current state of affairs in the United States, which is to say the article details the crisis and polarization that is ripping the country apart. A full-time worker whose taxable income is at the median currently earns about $50,000 a year. Yet had income been shared over the past 45 years as broadly as they were from the end of World War II until the early 1970s, that worker would instead be making $92,000 to $102,000.

Nick Hanauer, a venture capitalist and David Rolf, founder of Local 775 of the Service Employees International Union, funded the survey, which "explains why people are so pissed off. It explains why they are so economically precarious." RAND found that full-time, prime-age workers in the 25th percentile would be making $61,000 instead of $33,000 had everyone's earnings from 1975 to 2018 expanded roughly in line with gross domestic product, as they did during the 1950s and '60s. Workers in the 75th percentile would be at $126,000 instead of $81,000.

The survey shows the bottom 90 percent of American workers would be bringing home an additional $2.5 trillion in total annual income if economic gains were as equitably divided as they'd been in the past. Rolf calls it "the $2.5 trillion theft." The RAND data also makes clear who the winners from inequality are: those in the top one percent, the corporate elite that enthusiastically supported the off-shoring of jobs to China and Mexico starting back in the 1970s. If the economic pie had been divvied up since the mid-1970s like it was previously, yearly income for the average corporate elite would fall to $549,000.

The RAND survey found the basic pattern held true for part-time workers, entire families, men and women, Blacks and whites, urban dwellers and rural residents, and those with high school degrees and those with college diplomas. For the vast majority of Americans, what they earn at work through hourly wages or a salary represents practically all of their income. That is fully captured in the study.

RAND is generally viewed as taken seriously by the right and the left. Until now, nobody has teased out the bottom-line effects to individuals and their families of how economic growth is being shared across the income spectrum, thereby turning what can be an abstract concept into something much more tangible. Aside from "globalization," (i.e. offshoring of manual labor jobs) Hanauer and Rolf had no hesitation singling out culprits; allowing the minimum wage to deteriorate, overtime coverage to dwindle, and the effectiveness of labor law to decline, undermining union power. They also cite a shift in corporate culture that has elevated the interests of shareholders over those of workers, an ethos that took root around 50 years ago with the publication of an essay by University of Chicago economist Milton Friedman.

Many of these developments, Rolf points out, have been driven by the belief that an unfettered free market would generate wealth for everyone. Thanks to the RAND study, he says, "we now have the proof that this theory was wrong. This really is the entire country versus a very small number of very rich people."

CHAPTER 11

MONTREAL AND THE PRAIRIES

The more material things that we possess, the less clear life becomes. Therefore, if you want clarity, have a garage sale.
– Craig D. Lounsbrough

It seems the French and English have not gotten along well over the centuries, each nation invading the other as the opportunity arose. That enmity in Europe may no longer be as profound, but in North America it is different, or at least it was when I was born in Quebec. Montreal was in the middle of unprecedented cultural change in the late sixties, with French-speaking "seperatistes" engaging in violence and forcing the departure of much of the English-speaking minority. As an Anglo myself I went looking for work elsewhere and thankfully ended up in Vancouver in 1971. The population of Vancouver has since doubled, and the population of Toronto has tripled, but Montreal has lagged behind the national average growth rate for many reasons. Immigrants to Canada would rather live elsewhere. However, by 2030, the Greater Montreal Area is expected to grow to 5.275 million, of which 1.72 million will belong to a "visible minority group." One wonders how many of that minority will be Chinese.

The skyline of downtown Montreal has not changed much over the past 50 years.

FOLLOW THE MONEY: HOW CHINA BOUGHT THE WORLD

It has been fifty years since I was last in Montreal and while much has changed the overall appearance of the city has not. Unlike Vancouver there isn't a veritable wall of brand new glass towers cascading all over the landscape. I note the little wooden house where I was born in the suburb of St. Lambert, at one time a white clapboard cottage, is now restored and has a heritage designation. Google maps show many houses in the little town now possess back yard swimming pools, a sure sign of affluence. Property values are increasing.

While Canada remains a perennially popular destination for investment from China, shifting dynamics in Canada's national real estate market, brought about by economic and political forces, are seeing investors broaden their horizons. For many years, the story of Chinese real estate investment in Canada was a tale of only two cities, specifically Vancouver and Toronto. While those two major Canadian markets remain buoyant, various trends have forced Chinese investors to diversify their holdings, with Montreal "very much in vogue," notes a 2020 report from Juwai.com, the Chinese real estate evaluator. Canada's second-largest city also took the number three spot in volume of buyer inquiries, followed by Calgary, Ottawa, Belleville, Markham, Hamilton and Victoria rounding out the list.

In fact, Chinese investment in Canada is also spreading across the Prairies. With too few farms in China to feed a burgeoning population, Chinese immigrants have started buying up agricultural lands in Canada and shipping their produce to Asia. According to Fox News, with new overseas investment comes fears that a generation of young Canadian would-be farmers are being squeezed out of the market by newcomers that some suspect are being bankrolled by the government in Beijing. In Saskatchewan province, home to 45 percent of all arable land in Canada, the price of farmland has risen as much as 50 percent over three years in areas where Chinese immigrants have settled.

Provincial authorities there counted a half dozen large investment firms buying up farmlands in the province of one million people. For instance, Maxcrop is an upstart investment firm that deals in rural Saskatchewan real estate. Founded in 2009, the company owns 3,000 hectares (7,400 acres) and manages nearly 30,000 hectares for investors. A CBC report claims when wealthy Chinese national investors and Chinese immigrants begin to buy farmland in Canada, it directly impacts local farmers who have lived and farmed on their land for generations. Unlike in cities, where people from many different backgrounds are omnipresent, these farming communities are tight-knit, with many relatives living in the same small towns, sharing similar lifestyles.

Some provinces put strict limitations on the number of acres that foreign individuals or corporations can own in Canada. When immigrants who purchase farmland are labelled as foreign investors, it can create hostile relationships with the locals. The line is blurred when farmland is purchased by an immigrant who may or may not be financially backed by foreign investors. It's confusing for locals who don't understand where all the big money is really coming from. Foreign investment is increasing the price of land so much young families find themselves priced out of the housing market. The only locals who benefit are the retirees who sell their land to foreign investors, who are often the highest bidders.

The push to drain China's influence from the economy has reached America's farm country as well, as congressional lawmakers from both parties are looking at measures to crack down on foreign purchases of prime agricultural real estate. House lawmakers recently advanced legislation to that effect, warning that China's presence in the American food system poses a national security risk, and key Senate lawmakers have already shown interest in efforts to keep American farms in American hands. Chinese firms have expanded their presence in American agriculture over the last decade by snapping up farmland and purchasing major agribusinesses, like pork processing giant Smithfield Foods. By the start of 2020, Chinese owners controlled about 192,000 agricultural acres in the U.S., worth $1.9 billion, including land used for farming, ranching and forestry, according to the Agriculture Department.

USDA reported in 2018 that China's agricultural investments in other nations had grown more than tenfold since 2009. The Communist Party has actively supported investments in foreign agriculture as part of its "One Belt One Road" economic development plans, aiming to control a greater piece of China's food supply chain. Foreign investors by the end of 2019 held an interest in more than 35 million acres in the U.S., an area bigger than New York State. The total has grown by an average 2.3 million acres per year since 2015, according to USDA data. The money flowing into agricultural real estate from other countries also makes it difficult for new farmers in the U.S. to afford land as outside buyers bid up prices, and that poses a big risk with an older generation of farmers set to exit the industry.

CHINESE COMMUNIST APPOINTED TO CANADIAN SENATE

An article in the *Vancouver Sun* in 2016 revealed that Yuen Pau Woo, the former head of the Vancouver-based Asia Pacific Foundation of Canada, had been appointed to the Senate by Prime Minister Justin

Trudeau. (Senators are appointed, not elected.) This is another huge gaffe by the Prime Minister in relation to the CCP. Woo is widely regarded as a mouthpiece of the CCP in Canada. In his maiden speech to the Senate, Woo argued against a Senate motion that was critical of China's "escalating and hostile behaviour" in constructing artificial islands and military airfields on outcroppings in the South China Sea in order to assert its claimed sovereignty over resource-rich and strategically-vital areas.

Woo argued against the wisdom of wagging a judgmental finger at China. He said the provocative motion could worsen a tense situation involving what some analysts believe is one of the most dangerous geopolitical disputes in the world. "A dogmatic and trenchant insistence on international law could ... be the very precipitant of conflict," Woo cautioned fellow senators.

That was too much for the federal Conservatives, who had been blasting Trudeau for getting too close to China's Communist regime. "Canadians should be rightfully concerned that Justin Trudeau has appointed an apologist for the Chinese dictatorship in the Senate," said Tory MP Peter Kent in a statement that accused China of engaging in "unacceptable" behaviour in the region. "Woo ... used his very first speech in the Senate to deliver a message not on behalf of Canadians, but on behalf of Beijing. It seems every week we hear new evidence of the cozy relationship the Liberal government has with the Chinese Communist dictatorship. Now Liberals are using the Senate as a platform to undermine our allies and the foundation of international law."

On October 13, 2021 Woo attended a ceremony in Vancouver celebrating 72 years of Chinese Communist Party (CCP) rule. Attendees took photographs in front of opposing Chinese and Canadian flags shown on broadcasts on the Chinese government-linked channel Phoenix TV. The event was co-hosted by the Canadian Alliance of Chinese Associations and the Canada Sichuanese Friendship Association which both have associations with the CCP's foreign influence networks, the United Front.

CHAPTER 12

CALIFORNIA AND THE STATES

Capitalism is a social system owned by the capitalistic class, a small network of very wealthy and powerful businessmen, who compromise the health and security of the general population for corporate gain.
— Suzy Kassem

I t's been a few years since I was last in California. My family and I used to live in Marin County, just north of San Francisco. Marin is widely regarded as one of the best places to live in all of the "Excited States." High income, highly educated. There are a few dozen villages and one town scattered among rolling hills between San Francisco Bay and the Pacific Ocean. The hippies discovered Marin way back in the sixties and did their best to stop real estate developers from wrecking the place and turning it into ticky tacky suburbs. They did a good job. Musicians, "cultural creatives," software experts and "conservationists" all did so well to preserve the character of the county that it subsequently turned into some of the most expensive real estate in the country.

Back then, as a Canadian living with a wife who had an American passport I was somewhat limited in what kind of work I could do, so I wrote a feature story about real estate in the new village where we had moved and submitted it to the editor of the local newsmagazine, the prestigious *Pacific Sun*, an "alternative" weekly that had been published since the mid-sixties. The story was purchased and published immediately, and the editor wanted to know who the hell I was, only a month as a resident of the county and immediately an expert on housing? I explained I had been writing similar features in Vancouver newspapers. I said "nimbyism is everywhere," which is why it was so hard to get anything built in Marin. The "conservationists" had made it too difficult to build anything new for the past few decades, so the county was full of elderly widows living in four-bedroom houses because no one had been able to build any senior citizen retirement homes because of stringent development rules. I was hired by the *Sun* as a freelancer and spent much of my time for the next several years riding my mountain bike around the hills searching for waterfalls and picnic locations and then writing books about the secret places I discovered. Also, a couple of feature stories a month for the front cover were required. A tough assignment, but somebody has to do the hard jobs.

When not working my fingers to the bone, I commuted to San Francisco twice a week to play hockey. As a writer I don't do math, but I estimate in 7 years I made 700 trips to San Francisco, and after every game I parked my car in a new neighborhood and explored. I think I know the city better than anyone who lives there. The Mission District, where all the poor people and Latinos lived, was my favorite. Thanks to Google, rents there have quadrupled since I left. All the young techies working in Silicon Valley don't want to live in the Valley, or can't afford homes there. Many creative people from the Mission have been forced out and have moved to a neighborhood south of the Mission called Dogpatch, which is now getting yuppified. I visit Dogpatch on this trip and write about it as well.

Today I am making yet another exploration of the Golden State, this time on a family vacation from Vancouver. Living in California for seven years I had also enjoyed several hundred personal trips around the state. Since moving back to Canada the California Tourism Board invited me to come back "anytime, anywhere," so I continued my explorations of the state but

The cost of living in San Francisco and the Bay Area has skyrocketed with many new Chinese investments.

now as a tourist writing travel stories for Canadian newspapers. I wrote so many stories I ran out of ideas. The Tourism Board suggested I experience a "family tour of the finest hotels between San Francisco and Los Angeles," a hardship assignment that took my wife thirty seconds to agree with on my behalf. We wallowed in luxury at the Cavallo Point Lodge in Marin County, the Post Ranch Inn in Big Sur, the Beverly Hills Hilton and so on, but while "working" I kept my eye on real estate prices. We never bought a property in Marin because the prices were ridiculous until the crash of 2008 ruined the U.S. economy, by which time we had moved back to Canada.

On this trip I note the Golden State is proving to be the most popular of U.S. destinations for Chinese real estate investors, outranking New York with over 20 percent more buyers. A report on foreign investments issued by the National Association of Realtors (NAR) indicates 35 percent of China's $15 billion residential real estate investments in the U.S. are now in California, more than New York.

According to NAR's Housing and Commercial Research there is a long history of a large Chinese population in the Bay Area and Chinese are now the largest minority population in San Francisco. California also remains popular with Chinese investors because Silicon Valley is home to major software, Internet and tech companies such as Google, Intel, Facebook, Apple, Hewlett Packard, Twitter and others. California also has the highest fraction of Chinese buyers who are purchasing property for student use. Aside from San Francisco, investors are buying in cities such as San Diego, Los Angeles, San Jose, Fresno, and Sacramento. Among the other top U.S. destinations for Chinese investors is North Carolina, at 8 percent, Virginia at 7 percent, New Jersey at 6 percent, Texas at 5 percent, Florida at 4 percent, and Ohio at 3 percent. North Carolina's Raleigh and Austin in Texas are cities also known for their tech industries, while Cleveland, Ohio, has always had a large Chinese community. The NAR report shows single family homes account for about 62 percent of these investments, with about 48 percent of that number as primary residences.

According to the online news website Marco Polo, Chinese immigrants, homebuyers and real estate investors are transforming the Bay Area from San Francisco across the Bay to Oakland, and further south down the peninsula to the suburbs of Silicon Valley. In and around San Francisco are three megaprojects, all in poor neighborhoods and all started by rich Chinese immigrant investors. The money comes from the federal EB-5 program, which grants green cards to foreign investors and their families (around 80 percent of them Chinese) who invest $500,000 into any U.S.

113

Downtown San Francisco, seen in the background past the Golden Gate Bridge, has become one of the most expensive cities in the world in which to live

project that creates ten jobs. On the Oakland waterfront rises Brooklyn Basin, a massive 3,100-unit development on abandoned industrial land that languished for years. In the middle of the Bay is Treasure Island, the former home to Navy facilities where $155 million in EB-5 money is being used to fund 8,000 new homes. South of downtown San Francisco the massive San Francisco Shipyards project is under construction, 12,000 new homes and 5 million square feet of retail and office space, with over $300 million from EB-5 investors.

Turning toward downtown San Francisco, Oceanwide – a Chinese developer with $20 billion in assets and a string of U.S. projects from Honolulu to New York— is building a skyscraper slated to be the second tallest in the city. Nearby, China's second-largest property developer, Vanke, and its U.S. partner are building over 600 luxury condos overlooking the Bay Bridge. In a four-by-six block area downtown, five different Chinese developers are constructing over 1,000 new apartments and condos priced well above $1 million.

Finally, in Silicon Valley buyers from mainland China are snapping up multimillion dollar homes and paying entirely in cash. Chinese homebuyers recently topped lists of international buyers in the United States for the fourth straight year, spending $31.7 billion in one alone. Forty percent of those homes purchased were in California.

Meanwhile, driving the streets of San Francisco you can see homeless people everywhere, sleeping on the streets and in tents. There have always been homeless people in San Francisco, drawn by the tolerance of the citi-

zens for strange behavior and drug use, but the cost of living has skyrocketed like the skyscrapers that are popping up everywhere with Chinese money. I hear a new phrase I haven't heard before, the "working homeless." This
refers to teachers and other well-educated people who are fully employed
but poorly paid and can't afford to pay steep rents, so they are sleeping in
their cars and in tent cities. Since every new trend in America seems to ema-
nate from California, I guess it's only a matter of time before that new trend
arrives in many American cities. Heck, it's already happened in Vancouver,
where the only population growing faster than the homeless are the rich
Chinese snapping up multi-million dollar houses all over the city.

Living in Vancouver, I wasn't aware of the massive changes happening to my SF "second home." I thought only Vancouver was being overwhelmed with massive amounts of money being illegally smuggled into
the city while governments turned a blind eye and the cost of living went
through the roof. It's a good thing, I realize, that my wife and I already
own our home, even if it is only a condo. No matter how much money we
could earn, there is no possibility we could qualify for a mortgage in Vancouver. Only hockey and other sports players, rock stars and rich Chinese
immigrants can do that.

THE GIG ECONOMY

According to *Forbes Magazine*, more than one third (36 percent) of U.S.
workers have lost regular employment and are now forced to work in
the "Gig economy," which works out to a very large number of people, approximately 57 million if you are keeping track. With the rise of Uber, Lyft,
Etsy, Amazon Mechanical Turk, Freelancer.com, Ebay, and others, more
and more workers are doing part-time work, and "side hustles" as they are
often called, joining the gig economy as it is more formally known.

There are two types of gig workers. There are "independent" and "contingent" workers, the former being people who are truly their own "boss,"
and the latter being the group that work for another company just like a
regular employee might, of course minus the security and all the other benefits that come with being a full-fledged employee. Though gig workers get
many so-called "lifestyle benefits" (i.e. work when you want to) they fall
far behind on "traditional benefits" and in the "getting paid timely and ac-
curately" category. As you might expect, regular workers (those who are
employed full time) strongly agreed they get paid on time (82 percent),
but less than 70 percent of gig workers strongly agreed with that statement.

Peter Matthiessen

The Snow Leopard

CHAPTER THIRTEEN

TIBET AND INDIA

Earth provides enough to satisfy every man's needs, but not every man's greed.
— Mahatma Gandhi

It doesn't have an official name, but on my map it is shown as Bugu-la, the Tibetan word "la" indicating it is a pass through the mountains. In his epic book *The Snow Leopard,* (1978) naturalist and travel writer Peter Matthiessen estimated the elevation at 16,900 feet. Here, in the northwest region of Nepal known as Upper Dolpo, the Tibetan plateau far below stretches as an endless series of barren mountains, a sight few people in history have ever seen. I am on a mission to replicate Matthiessen's epic journey he took back in 1973. His trekking party had a group photo taken at the top of this very pass by colleague George Schaller (published in his book *Stones of Silence,* 1980), so I take one myself. Since I am all alone atop Bugu-la, in one of the most remote places in the world, there is no one shown in the photo.

At one time Upper Dolpo was a region of Tibet, until the warlike Nepalese Ghurkas marched in and took possession for themselves. The region, along with the nearby Tibetan culture of Mustang, still belongs to Nepal. Cut off from the rest of the world by the Himalayas, Upper Dolpo and Mustang contain the last remnants of pure Tibetan culture left on the planet. Since there are no minerals or natural resources in Upper Dolpo (it is above the tree line) the region remains undisturbed.

Our mission, led by a Tibetan monk, is to "find and rescue abandoned children living in the world's highest inhabited villages, bring them to India where they can get an education, and eventually they will return to Upper Dolpo as teachers and doctors and save the last vestiges of their ancient Tibetan culture." Being as there is a civil war ongoing in Nepal at the time, and I have already been captured by the Maoist guerillas and paid a ransom to be released, I am somewhat apprehensive about accidentally crossing the border into Tibet by mistake, there being no checkpoints or people or any living thing in this vast wilderness.

Being captured by the Chinese army would be worse than being robbed by the Nepalese Maoists.

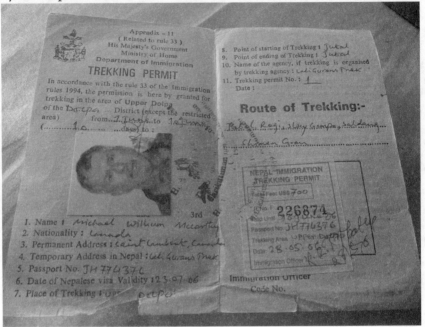

The author required a special permit to trek to the Upper Dolpo district of northwest Nepal, the highest inhabited region in the entire world, but one with threats from the Chinese army.

It seems that many people around the world have forgotten that Tibet was once a sovereign nation, with its own long history, culture and language. The People's Liberation Army of China's illegal and immoral invasion in 1959 led to years of murder that culminated in the complete overthrow of the Tibetan government and the self-imposed exile of the Dalai Lama to India along with 100,000 Tibetans. According to a study undertaken by the University of Massachusetts, since the invasion over a million Tibetans have been killed in Tibet. With the Chinese policy of resettlement of ethnic Chinese to Tibet, the Tibetans have become a minority in their own country. Chinese is now the official language.

Compared to pre-1959 levels, only a handful of monks are still allowed to practice their religion, under the Chinese government's strict watch. Up to 6,000 monasteries and shrines were destroyed in the Chinese Cultural Revolution. Famines have appeared for the first time in recorded history, natural resources are being devastated, and wildlife depleted to extinction. Tibetan culture itself is coming close to being eradicated.

Many of the native Khampa people of eastern Tibet fled to northern Nepal when Tibet was invaded. Aided by the CIA they started a series of raids and attacks on Chinese troops, but they never had any chance of defeating the mighty Chinese army. The Khampas mostly camped in the Nepali district of Mustang, in the Kali Gendaki Gorge just east of Upper Dolpo. No sign can be found of their involvement today, and there is little threat of any invasion of Nepal by the CCP. However, since 2008 Chinese investments in the Himalayan state haves surged, and by 2014 China outranked nearby India for the first time in terms of total investment. China's strategic financial inclination towards Nepal is evident from these statistics, and it is a serious challenge to India in its own territory.

China's funding is evident across major infrastructure and energy projects in Nepal. These include the West Seti Dam, the Pokhara Airport and Upper Trishuli hydropower project. In return, Nepal has agreed to extend its cooperation to the Silk Road Economic Belt, part of China's ambitious One Belt One Road initiative. Infrastructure funding with cultural overtones is part of China's play in Nepal. The (atheist) Chinese government-funded Asia-Pacific Exchange and Cooperation Foundation plans to invest $3 billion to convert Lumbini, the birthplace of Buddha, into a "cultural zone" that will attract millions of Buddhist pilgrims and tourists from around the world.

Since the CCP invasion in 1959, peaceful demonstrations and protests by nuns, monks, and Tibetan laypeople have resulted in hundreds of thousands of arrests in Tibet. Political prisoners are tortured and held in sub-standard conditions. There is no freedom of speech, religion, or press and arbitrary dissidents continue to be incarcerated. Forced abortion, sterilization of Tibetan women and the transfer of low income Chinese citizens to Tibet threaten the survival of Tibet's unique and ancient culture. In some Tibetan provinces, Chinese settlers outnumber Tibetans 7 to 1. Within China itself, of course, massive human rights abuses continue. It is estimated up to twenty million Chinese citizens work in prison camps, especially Uighers of Muslim faith in northwest China, incarcerated in "re-education camps" where they produce cotton goods for western consumers at discount prices.

Most of the Tibetan plateau lies above 14,000 feet. Tibet is the source of five of Asia's greatest rivers, on which over 2 billion people depend for survival. Since 1959, the Chinese government estimates that they have removed over $54 billion worth of timber in Tibet. Over 80 percent of the forests have been destroyed and large amounts of Chinese nuclear and toxic waste has been disposed of in Tibet. Despite these facts and figures, U.S. corporations continue to support China economically, even in Uigher territory.

The atheist Chinese Community Party, as an excuse to invade their neighbor and pillage its natural resources, made up a cock and bull story about Tibet historically being a province of theirs. This must have come as a shock to the Tibetans, a devout people with their own religion, language and history. The understanding that China invades its neighbors by making vague excuses should be of great interest to those concerned about the future of the South China Sea, where the Communist Party threatens to invade and "take back" Taiwan, a country where they never set foot and have no legal claim.

In Nepal, the Snow Leopard trek of mine involves 20 days of walking 500 miles in a vast circle, much above 15,000 feet in elevation, through Upper Dolpo and back again to Lower Dolpo. Since Upper Dolpo used to be part of Tibet, there is always the concern that the Chinese might want to "take it back," but unlike Hong Kong and Taiwan there is little of material value in rocky and desolate Upper Dolpo to the CCP leaders. However, in other nearby border regions the Chinese are up to their old tricks, trying to add other people's territory to their own.

Beginning in 2020, Chinese and Indian troops engaged in aggressive melees, face-offs, and skirmishes at locations along the Sino-Indian border, in Ladakh and the Tibet Autonomous Region, and near the border between Sikkim and the Tibet Autonomous Region. Additional clashes also took place at locations in eastern Ladakh along the Line of Actual Control (LAC). Chinese forces objected to Indian road construction in the Galwan river valley. According to Indian sources, melees resulted in the deaths of several Chinese and Indian soldiers. For the first time in 45 years, shots were fired along the LAC.

Amid the standoff, India reinforced the region with approximately 12,000 additional workers, who would assist in completing the development of Indian highway infrastructure along the Sino-Indian border. Following the Galwan Valley skirmish, several Indian campaigns boycotting Chinese products were started. Action on the economic front included cancellation and additional scrutiny of certain contracts with Chinese firms, and calls were also made to stop the entry of Chinese companies into strategic markets in India. The Indian government banned over 200 Chinese digital apps, including those owned by Alibaba, Tencent, Baidu, Sina, and Bytedance.

The view of Tibet from 16,900 feet in northwest Nepal is one of endless cold and barren peaks marching off into the distance.

After 22 days trekking in Upper Dolpo, crossing several high passes of 18,000 feet, I return to "civilization," if the anarchy of the capital city of Kathmandu may be described as such. The newspapers are full of stories about Chinese troops provoking Indian troops along the border. Given that the Indian army is huge, there is no chance the Chinese will invade that particular neighbor, but a few war games are good practice for the Indian troops for when the real thing comes along.

EXECUTIONS

According to Wikipedia (oh, no, not Wikipedia again!) capital punishment in China is an approved legal penalty. It is commonly applied for murder and drug trafficking, although it is also a penalty for various other offenses. Executions are carried out by lethal injection or by shooting. The majority of Chinese people support capital punishment, although the government (i.e. the CCP) does not bother to seek any public approval. That would be tantamount to democracy.

In 2022, the World Coalition Against the Death Penalty announced that since 2007, on average at least 8,000 people were executed in China per year. By both confirmed and estimated data, the number of executions from capital punishment in China is far higher than any other country. Chinese courts have a "guilty verdict" 99 percent of the time, so there's no need to waste money on a lawyer.

Lethal injection is more commonly used for "economic crimes" such as corruption, while firing squads are used for more common crimes like murder. Because demand is high for execution and building facilities can be expensive, the state often deploys special "death wagons," police buses designed to administer the injection. After the 1997 decision to legalize lethal injection, CCP officials began using execution vans across China. Becoming popular in 2007, officials state that the vans are cost-effective by allowing communities without the money to build dedicated death rows to kill prisoners easily.

Usually a converted 24-seat bus, the execution van maintains the appearance of a normal police van on the outside with no markings indicating its sinister purpose. The rear of the vehicle houses a windowless chamber where the execution takes place. Several cameras are present and feed closed-circuit televisions in the front of the van; a recording can be made if desired. The bed itself slides out of the wall under its own power, on which the convicted person is strapped down. A syringe is put into the arm by a technician and a police official administers the injection by pressing a button.

Aside from executions, organ harvesting is also big these days under the CCP. According to an article in *Forbes* magazine in June 2021, a group of U.N. independent experts expressed their concerns at allegations of organ harvesting carried out on minority groups in China including Falun Gong practitioners, Uyghurs, Tibetans, Muslims and Christians in detention in China. According to the statement, the experts received "credible information that detainees from ethnic, linguistic or religious minorities may be forcibly subjected to blood tests and organ examinations such as ultrasound and x-rays, without their informed consent. The results of the examinations are reportedly registered in a database of living organ sources that facilitates organ allocation."

The statement further indicated that "according to the allegations received, the most common organs removed from the prisoners are reportedly hearts, kidneys, livers, corneas and, less commonly, parts of livers. This form of trafficking with a medical nature allegedly involves health sector professionals, including surgeons, anesthetists and other medical specialists."

An article in NBC News in 2019 states that the organs of members of marginalized groups detained in Chinese prison camps are being forcefully harvested, sometimes when patients are still alive, an international tribunal sitting in London has concluded. Some of the more than 1.5 million detainees in Chinese prison camps are being killed for their organs to serve a booming transplant trade that is worth some $1 billion a year, concluded the China Tribunal, an independent body tasked with investigating organ harvesting from prisoners of conscience in the authoritarian state. "Forced organ harvesting has been committed for years throughout China on a significant scale," the tribunal concluded in its final judgment. The practice is "of unmatched wickedness – on a death for death basis – with the killings by mass crimes committed in the last century."

The website China Justice Observer reports there are 42 crimes for which the death penalty is meted out. You might think murder or drug dealing would top the list but no; the top ten crimes are political. The criminal offences eligible for the death penalty are Betrayal of the Country, Armed Rebellion and Rioting, Collaborating with the Enemy and Betrayal, Spying or Espionage. Plus stealing, spying, buying, and illegally providing state secrets and intelligence abroad; Providing material support to the enemy; Arson, flooding, explosions, and spreading hazardous substances.

The astute observer might note that eight of the ten are threats to the "state," better described as the CCP itself, because the Party controls everything in China. Any of the eight so-called "serious crimes" can be applied to anyone dissenting with the Party's views. It's impossible to know how many of the executions in China are for murder or violence, or simply for political reasons or dissent. Observers prone to irony could point out that the State itself could be charged with flooding, because the 3 Gorges Dam project caused the displacement of 1.3 million people and the destruction of many natural features and countless rare architectural and archaeological sites. As for "spreading hazardous substances," the pollution in China is so extreme you can't breathe the air. According to the estimates by GLOBOCAN 2018, about 4,285,033 new cancer cases were diagnosed in China in 2018 alone.

CHAPTER 14

DUBAI IS THE FUTURE

Among the rich you will never find a really generous man even by acci-dent. They may give their money away, but they will never give them-selves away; they are egotistic, secretive, dry as old bones. To be smart enough to get all that money you must be dull enough to want it."
— G.K. Chesterton, *A Miscellany of Men*

After I went to Dubai in the United Arab Emirates on a press trip I titled my subsequent story "Dubai is the future." Where once was nothing but sand now there are gigantic skyscrapers. Dubai has the world's largest indoor shopping mall, world's highest building, world's largest indoor ski hill, world's largest man-made islands, and soon will have the world's largest airport. The local sheiks have done nothing to deserve such vast wealth; they simply sit atop a vast sea of oil that Allah has kindly provided for them, obviously his chosen people. Foreigners come to work the oil fields, run the local businesses and staff the hospi-tality industry. The sheiks spend their ill-gotten wealth on fast cars, wild parties and (cleverly) installing solar panels that will replace oil when it finally runs out.

Dubai has evolved from sandy desert to a vast sea of glistening downtown skyscrapers.

Why is Dubai the future? It needs to be understood that recent super powers like the United States, Russia, Germany and Great Britain are in decline for various reasons. The Brits no longer "rule the waves," America is no longer the world's police officer, and Germany regrets being duped by Putin the Poisoner into thinking the Russians were trustworthy. Coming in to partly replace these former powers are the Middle East oil kingdoms, and of course China, which is rolling in dough thanks to its lop-sided trade deal with the United States.

The view from the observation deck on the 148th floor of the Barj Khalifa is mindboggling. The Barj at 2,716 feet is the world's tallest building. Far below, looking like pin pricks, are the usual 40-50 story high rise office towers. Offshore, contractors are building more and more man-made islands for sale to the richest people in the world. Invisible to the naked eye is the vast amount of money invested in Dubai and the Middle East by new Chinese investors.

After coming home to Canada, I do some research. According to an investment website titled The First Group, Chinese investments in Dubai real estate hit $384 million U.S. in 2014, an annual increase of more than 300 percent, according to the Dubai Land Department (DLD). In the first eight months of 2015 the figure had already reached $326 million. The Chinese were the sixth biggest foreign investors in Dubai after Indians, British, Iranians, Canadians, and Russians. The top 10 list also includes Americans, the French, and Afghanis. The rich, ultra-rich, and robber barons from other nations know where is best to hide their money.

At the time of my visit there were 4,200 Chinese enterprises operating in Dubai and around 200,000 Chinese expats, according to the China Centre for International Economic Exchanges. In the future, more than half a million Chinese could move here, said the centre's Executive Vice Chairman Zhang Xiaoqiang. According to a report in the *South China Morning Post*, traditionally the United Arab Emirates (UAE) was not a likely destination for Chinese property investment until it emerged as a regional hub for the Belt and Road Initiative (BRI). China spent $71.1 billion U.S. in the Middle East between 2014 and 2017 as part of the BRI, and has pledged to invest a further $10.7 billion U.S. by 2022 in Oman's Special Economic Zone at Duqm. Traditionally, the United Arab Emirates (UAE) was not a likely destination for Chinese property investment, until it emerged as a regional hub for the Belt and Road Initiative (BRI). By the end of 2021, the UAE was the eighth most popular destination searched for on Chinese property portal juwai.com. Inquiries were up 43 per cent on the year before, but had quadrupled over a two-year basis, according to the company. On LuxuryEstate.com, the emirate of Dubai is currently the 12th most searched destination by Chinese users following a 44 per cent increase in inquiries in 2020.

LuxuryEstate.com notes that the UAE government offers residency to foreigners who buy properties. The duration of the visa is directly related to the property value. They have highly favorable tax conditions: there are no property taxes nor stamp duties, and this applies to all properties, even the most expensive. Local authorities recently introduced a retire-ment visa and that will probably contribute to boost the luxury property market in the future.

On the press trip we western scribes are treated to 7-star luxury, fine meals and limo tours (air conditioned, of course). We go "dune bashing" in the deep sands of the Empty Quarter, a stupid and dangerous prac-tice that sees huge SUVs flying over the top of giant sand dunes. We visit mosques, the huge shopping malls and a hockey rink and even the souk (old town market) that is fairly new by Middle Eastern standards but al-ready left in the dust by sparkling new attractions. It is so hot that to step outside the car for more than a minute risks hospitalization.

In the midst of the tour an opportunity arises to visit the "world's most expensive hotel suite." This turns out to be the Royal Suite at the Atlantis Hotel on the Palm Islands, at $57,000 U.S. per night (at the time of my

At $57,000 U.S. per night the Royal Suite at the Atlantis Hotel is the most expensive hotel suite in the world.

visit) the most expensive in the world. There are only three bedrooms, but enough space in the living and dining rooms to "party over 100 people," according to our guide. He notes we are lucky to have a quick peek because the Royal Suite is booked solid every day of the year. Who books the suite, I ask? Rich Arabs and world famous celebrities is the reply. Why, Kim Kardashian had been a guest the night before, with friends! I bounced on the bed to see if it still worked, a line that was removed by my editor in my feature article when it was published.

U.S. STATE OF EMERGENCY

Thomas Homer-Dixon is executive director of the Cascade Institute at Royal Roads University. His latest book is Commanding Hope: The Power We Have to Renew a World in Peril. This is an excerpt from an essay of his about the impending collapse of American democracy.

"By 2025, American democracy could collapse, causing extreme domestic political instability, including widespread civil violence. By 2030, if not sooner, the country could be governed by a right-wing dictatorship. We mustn't dismiss these possibilities just because they seem ludicrous or too horrible to imagine. In 2014, the suggestion that Donald Trump would become president would also have struck nearly everyone as absurd. But today we live in a world where the absurd regularly becomes real and the horrible commonplace."

Myself, in the 1980s I sometimes listened to Rush Limbaugh, the American right-wing radio talk show host and later an unsuccesful television personality. I remarked to friends at the time that, with each broadcast, it was if Mr. Limbaugh were wedging the sharp end of a chisel into a faint crack in the moral authority of U.S. political institutions, and then slamming the other end of that chisel with a hammer. In 2020, President Donald Trump awarded Mr. Limbaugh the Presidential Medal of Freedom. The act signalled that Mr. Limbaugh's brand of bullying, populist white ethnocentrism – a rancid blend of aggrieved attacks on liberal elites, racist dog-whistling, bragging about American exceptionalism and appeals to authoritarian leadership – had become an integral part of mainstream political ideology in the U.S.

Some of these infantile rants can be traced to the country's founding; an abiding distrust in government baked into the country's political culture during the Revolution, to slavery, to the political compromise of the Electoral College that slavery spawned, to the overrepresentation of rural voting power in the Senate, and to the failure of Reconstruction after the Civil War. But successful polities around the world have overcome flaws just as fundamental.

As "returns" to labor have stagnated (i.e wage increases) and returns to capital have soared, much of the "middle" of the U.S. population has fallen behind. Inflation-adjusted wages for the median male worker in the fourth quarter of 2019 were lower than in 1979; meanwhile, between 1978 and 2016, CEO incomes in the biggest companies rose from 30 times that of the average worker to 271 times. Economic insecurity is widespread in broad swaths of the country's interior, while growth is increasingly concentrated in a dozen or so metropolitan centres.

Two other material factors are key. Right-wing ideologues have inflamed fears that traditional U.S. culture is being erased and whites are being "replaced." The second is pervasive elite selfishness. The wealthy and powerful in America are broadly unwilling to pay taxes, invest in the public services, or create the avenues for vertical mobility that would lessen their country's economic, educational, racial and geographic gaps. The more an under-resourced government can't solve everyday problems, the more people give up on it, and the more they turn to their own resources and their own narrow identity groups for safety.

Chinese Foreign Direct Investments in Africa

In millions of dollars, 2019

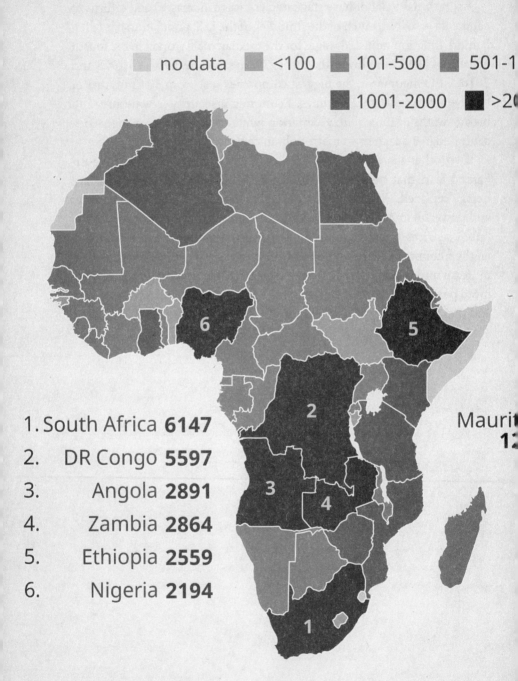

no data   <100   101-500   501-1

1001-2000   >20

1. South Africa **6147**
2. DR Congo **5597**
3. Angola **2891**
4. Zambia **2864**
5. Ethiopia **2559**
6. Nigeria **2194**

Mauri
1

 Source: Johns Hopkins University SAIS China-Africa Research

CHAPTER FIFTEEN

OUT OF AFRICA

When morality comes up against profit, it is seldom that profit loses.
— Shirley Chisholm

A frica is one of the few places in the world where I have never been. Friends who have lived there tell me the same Chinese invasion of money and people in Vancouver and many western cities is happening there as well. I had heard that the Chinese Communist Party was heavily investing in Africa, buying land and planting crops, building infrastructure and digging great holes in the ground. This is true, say my business friends. In fact, China is not really "investing." It's actually a system of concessional loans. Nearly all of all China's programs in Africa contain a clause that stipulates all infrastructure-related programs are required to have 70 percent Chinese workers. The African governments can choose where the infrastructure is built, but they have to pay back the money in the form of natural resources, and are required to give employment to hundreds of thousands of Chinese workers instead of Africans.

As part of Chinese "investments," Africans are discovering that China is dumping its own cheap manufactured consumer goods on African markets, forcing small African businesses into bankruptcy, since they cannot afford to sell goods at the same prices. An estimated 750,000 Chinese have migrated to Africa over the past decade and millions more are on their way. Nigeria, Angola, Ethiopia and Sudan have received 70 percent of Chinese funds designated to Africa. That's because they have the raw resources that China wants. The Chinese Communist Party leaders are building roads to take raw minerals out of Africa. In exchange for building the infrastructure, they have negotiated under-market prices for Africa's oil, timber, coal, copper, and coltan.

The Chinese government is deliberately creating segregated neighbourhoods in Africa for Chinese people only. Chinatowns have sprung up throughout the continent. They are paying African workers very low salaries. Despite being able to get all the necessary timber for its internal

China supplies dictators in Africa with weapons and money to keep those dictators in power while China strip mines those countries of their natural resources.
Photo courtesy of Unsplash

market at home in China, the Chinese officials have signed contracts to get 70 percent of its timber imports from Africa. Chinese firms are not respecting conservation laws, wiping out whole forests throughout Gabon, Cameroon, Congo-Kinshasa, Equatorial Guinea and Liberia. China is the number one weapons supplier to Africa. From Ethiopia, Sudan, and Congo to Zimbabwe, Cameroon or Gabon, China is selling African leaders weapons they can use against their own people. Countries like Zimbabwe or Sudan, where people are most affected by extreme poverty, have received the harshest loan conditions possible. The entire continent is being raped, and the world pays no attention.

China, Africa's biggest foreign investor, has more at stake in Zimbabwe, and more political influence, than any other state. This is largely due to its extensive investments in the mining, agriculture, energy and construction sectors. China was Zimbabwe's top trade partner in 2015, buying 28 percent of its exports. But the Chinese connection is about more than money. The pre-independence guerrilla force led to victory by Robert Mugabe, the Zimbabwean president who finally died at age 93, was financed and armed by the Chinese in the 1970s. Close ties between the nations have continued. When the U.S. and E.U. imposed sanctions after Zimbabwe's 2002 elections, China stepped in, investing in over 100 projects. Beijing also blocked UN Security Council moves to impose an arms embargo and restrictions on regime figures. Xi Jinping, China's president, visited Zimbabwe in December 2015 and has since promised a massive $5 billion in additional direct aid and investment. Jinping described China as Zimbabwe's "all-weather friend."

Jinping's personal support extended to providing $46 million towards constructing a new parliament building in Harare. Aware of criticism from Mugabe's opponents that Beijing was propping up a despotic regime, China used soft power tools to win over public opinion. This included a $100 million medical loan facility in 2011 and the construction of a new hospital in rural Zimbabwe. In 2015, state-owned Power Construction Corporation of China signed a $1.2-billion deal to expand Zimbabwe's largest thermal power plant. Chinese investors have also bought into farms seized from their former white owners and given to Mugabe cronies who subsequently neglected them. China financed and built Zimbabwe's National Defence College and the People's Liberation Army has helped train the Zimbabwean army. The future of the Dark Continent is not bright at all.

COERCION OF EMIGRANTS

In an article in the *Globe and Mail*, RCMP commissioner Brenda Lucki calls Beijing's interference and intimidation operations targeting people who emigrate from China to Canada a "problem," and says victims can report the harassment to Canadian authorities without fear. Commissioner Lucki said that she had no details at hand about the scale of the issue, but is looking to step up actions the force takes against such operations. "I would say yes, it is a problem, but the breadth and depth of it I couldn't really say for sure."

"It's a growing problem, obviously, and something we want to work together with our international and domestic partners on. A lot of it is about awareness and education, because things happen and we want to make sure people who are affected by this feel safe – that they can report this without fear of reprisal."

To that end, Commissioner Lucki said, there is an RCMP phone number for people affected by such incidents to call. She said the number has been available at least since she became commissioner in 2018, but she could not immediately say how many people have called it.

The *Globe and Mail* reported that China has been expanding its use of coercion to force the return of Chinese citizens who have settled abroad, many of them in Australia, Canada and the United States, in a campaign targeting fugitives and dissidents.

The trend was identified in a new report by Spain-based rights group Safeguard Defenders. Citing Chinese government data, Safeguard's report says Beijing had surpassed 10,000 returns under one repatriation program, called Sky Net, by late 2021. This is the only program for which data are available, and the watchdog group says it is just the tip of the iceberg when it comes to non-judicial efforts to secure the return of people wanted by the Chinese state in 120 countries.

The report identifies three methods China employs to forcibly retrieve citizens. Chinese authorities first attempt to coax a return through the target's family and relatives who still live in China. They harass loved ones and try to coerce them into passing messages to the person abroad. A second method is directly approaching the target outside mainland China, including by sending Chinese agents. A third method is what Safeguard Defenders calls "kidnappings abroad," in which Chinese authorities arrest targets on foreign soil and take them back to China.

Cherie Wong, the executive director of Alliance Canada Hong Kong, an umbrella group for Hong Kong pro-democracy activists in Canada, said many have lost faith that law enforcement in this country can help stop harassment from Beijing. "The community has lost trust in Canadian agencies to help them. Many individuals have approached RCMP for help, but are bounced between enforcement and intelligence agencies who do not have the tools and resources to effectively counter foreign interference operations. Chinese party-state actors have long utilized legal grey areas to assert influence inappropriately."

Ivy Li, a spokesperson for the Canadian Friends of Hong Kong, said Canada needs a foreign-agents registration act like those in Australia or the United States, as well as a centralized reporting centre for victims of intimidation by the Chinese government. Mehmet Tohti, executive director of the Uyghur Rights Advocacy Project, said the RCMP does not have a public record of successfully tackling foreign-based harassment in Canada. "Uyghurs and other China-related activists approached the RCMP numerous times without any tangible result. For that reason many activists have already stopped reporting to the RCMP," he said. He added that he personally tried after his organization's smartphones were hacked. His legal adviser was directed from one unit to another unit, one department to another department.

Former RCMP commissioner Bob Paulson has acknowledged that not enough is being done to stop coercion activities by China in Canada. Mr. Paulson, the commissioner from 2011 to 2017, told the *Globe* that Canadian laws relating to extortion and threatening behaviour forbid these activities. But, he said: "We hadn't devoted resources to this. I can't think of an instance where we have succeeded on the back of a complaint that Chinese agents were strong-arming citizens. You have to throw your shoulder into it."

CHAPTER 16

THE KILLING FIELDS OF CAMBODIA

A farm worker greets Josef Stalin at his potato farm. "Comrade Stalin, we have so many potatoes that piled one on top of the other, they would reach all the way to God," the farmer excitedly tells his leader. "But God does not exist," replies Stalin. "Exactly," says the farmer. "Neither do the potatoes."

After pillaging Indochina of its rubber, tin and other resources – and commencing a profitable heroin trade - the French left Cambodia to its own devices in the 1950s, leaving a small trail behind consisting of some Art Deco architecture, fine coffee and tasty baguettes. I am sitting on the patio of a café in the capital of Phnom Penh near the Mekong River enjoying a coffee and pastry while ignoring a monk attempting to bully me into making a financial donation to his begging bowl. I am also reading the *Cambodia Daily* newspaper and attempting to ascertain the future of this poor country, if such a thing is possible while drinking a coffee and wondering what adventures I might enjoy while here on my latest trip to this destitute country.

I have already re-visited CCH, the Centre for Children's Happiness, an "orphanage" on the outskirts of the city, where founder Mech Sokha runs a home for children rescued from Steung Meanchey, the gigantic town dump. At CCH I conspired to induce a rich Canadian friend to pay for the installation of Internet service and am therefore feeling smug with myself. Also, I have been hot on the trail of the infamous journalist Bernie Krisher, whom I met in San Francisco and who has become something of a mentor to me in my attempts to learn and practice global micro-philanthropy on my trips to poor countries around the world.

The name of Bernie Krisher strikes fear in the hearts of many. As a Jewish child he escaped death during the Holocaust in Germany. As the American bureau chief for *Newsweek* in Asia during the Vietnam War he met and interviewed Presidents and Emperors, building up a huge rolodex of powerful contacts. He launched a tabloid that revolutionized Japanese media. In "retirement," Bernie became a humanitarian, flouting international sanctions to bring rice to starving North Korea and pouring vast sums into war-ravaged Cambodia. There he built hundreds of schools, founded an orphanage and a hospital, and started the *Cambodia Daily*. Krisher relentlessly pumped his connections for money and started project after project, from starting the schools to an initiative that paid families to educate their daughters.

In 1993 Krisher started his English-and-Khmer-language *Daily News* out of an old hotel on the Mekong riverfront. He enticed a few ex-pat Americans to run it, and they recruited Cambodian staffers who worked as fixers or translators. In a country where the local press was mostly corrupt or partisan, the paper (whose motto was "All the news without fear or favor") aimed to embody objective journalism, and to train a generation of journalists.

The Cambodia government has now forced a shutdown of the *Daily*, which, despite its tiny circulation of about 5,000, had been the paper of record for Cambodia's civil society. Its reporters had regularly broken news that the rest of the country's media then followed. The recent closure was part of a broad crackdown on Cambodia's independent press and institutions, one that would in short order see the opposition leader jailed and multiple watchdog groups shuttered. The bank accounts of Krisher's charities were frozen, and the editors threatened with arrest.

Although 90 percent of eligible voters participated in the UN-administered 1993 elections, Cambodian democracy got off to a rocky start and remains so. The royalists, led by Sihanouk's son Prince Norodom Ranariddh, got the most votes, but Hun Sen's Cambodian People's Party, which came in second, refused to accept the result. After a standoff, Ranariddh and Hun Sen were made co–prime ministers, until such time Hun Sen got rid of the competition. A bloodless coup had taken place and Hun Sen remains the Prime Minister to this day.

The Daily was not the only media outlet targeted. Radio stations broadcasting *Radio Free Asia* and *Voice of America*, U.S.-backed services that provide independent news to many rural Cambodians, were shuttered, as was the U.S.-funded National Democratic Institute. The international community, wary of a return to civil war, has looked away. Today, with the assistance of the Chinese Communist Party, Hun Sen runs the country with an iron fist.

According to Sam Rainsey, the co-founder and acting leader of the opposition Cambodia National Rescue Party, writing in *The Strategist* online

The author explores the huge garbage dump known as Steung Meanchey in Phnom Penh, home to thousands of poverty stricken people picking bits and pieces of garbage to sell.

magazine, it has long been feared that Cambodia's growing dependence on China—its largest aid donor, investor and creditor—would lead to a Chinese military presence in the country. According to a *Wall Street Journal* report, those fears are now true.

"Like a gambler reliant on a loan shark," writes Rainsey, Cambodia has in recent years racked up massive, opaque debts to China that it cannot repay. This has given China considerable leverage. Judging by China's history of "debt-trap diplomacy," which it employs in "developing countries," it was only a matter of time before the Chinese Communist Party used its leverage over Cambodia to strengthen its regional military posture. China and Cambodia have secretly signed an agreement giving China exclusive rights to a part of Cambodia's naval base on the Gulf of Thailand.

Rainsey says the Cambodian people are fed up with the authoritarian and corrupt leadership of the world's longest-serving prime minister. The regime has so far countered any resistance by cracking down hard on dissent. In the last sham election, Hun Sen's Cambodian People's Party won every seat in the parliament after dissolving the leading opposition party, the Cambodia National Rescue Party (of which Rainsey is co-founder and acting leader).

The coastal naval base will provide a convenient springboard for China to bully or even attack nearby countries, thereby enhancing its ability to assert its territorial claims and economic interests in the South China Sea. China's tightening control over trade routes through which one-third of the world's shipping passes raises obvious risks for the U.S. and Europe.

Chinese dominance in the South China Sea will also go a long way towards entrenching China as a global naval superpower, with investments in ports as far afield as Greece, Israel, Italy and the Horn of Africa. The Cambodian base will complete a Chinese military perimeter around mainland Southeast Asia that leaves the entire region under China's thumb. Pakistan, Sri Lanka and Vanuatu all have the potential for deep-water ports that could serve Chinese naval expansion and restrict Western access to key parts of the Indian and Pacific Oceans. Already, China has courted all three countries with long-term financial aid packages.

The Buddhist monk fixing me with a deadly stare this morning finally gives up and moves on to bully other victims, just as China under the rule of the CCP has moved into the region to bully and intimidate Indochina. It may be time for western nations to wake up and smell the coffee and discover what is happening in Southeast Asia since the Americans forces fled Vietnam, just the way they more recently ran from Afghanistan. Nature, just like ruthless politicians, abhors a vacuum.

Chinese investments in Cambodia do nothing to improve the lives of tens of thousands of children living and begging on the streets of Phnom Penh

140

THE CCP AND THE GLOBAL CHINESE DIASPORA

Excerpted from an article by Dr. Oscar Almen of the Swedish Defence Research Agency, May 2021.

Concern about China's growing international influence has deepened in recent years. Part of this concern involves China's ability to mobilize the Chinese diaspora outside of the People's Republic of China (PRC). The CCP seeks to extend its authoritarian rule to the Chinese diaspora abroad as a way to gain support for its policies and reduce the influence of its opponents. A crucial aspect is the question of whom the Chinese party-state regards as Chinese and thus a legitimate target for its influence operations.

Opponents risk being threatened or abducted. China's extraterritorial activities have various security consequences including Chinese state influence in domestic politics of foreign states, security threats against foreign citizens of Chinese descent and an undermining of principles of nationality in international law. China does not recognize dual nationality. Consequently, Chinese who acquire foreign citizenship are no longer considered Chinese citizens by the PRC. However, the Chinese leadership uses ethnic and racial references when talking about the Chinese people and continually emphasizes the importance of bloodline and heritage.

According to this view, all foreign nationals with Chinese heritage, regardless of how many generations ago their families left China, can potentially be included in the CCP's idea of the Chinese nation. At the seventh Conference of Friendship of Overseas Chinese Associations in 2014, Xi Jinping said, "There are tens of millions of overseas Chinese in the world, and everyone is a member of the Chinese family." This perspective obscures the distinction between Chinese nationals abroad (huaqiao) and foreign nationals of Chinese heritage (huaren) specified under PRC law. The CCP expects overseas Chinese to be patriotic and loyal to what it considers to be their ancestral homeland.

The Chinese diaspora has been declared an important part of the process of rejuvenating the Chinese nation. The overseas Chinese affairs work, led by the United Front Work Department (UFWD), has intensified its efforts to mobilize the Chinese diaspora, regardless of citizenship, for the CCP's cause. Chinese actors with different degrees of involvement with the CCP have been active in influencing politics in Western democracies such as Australia.

Swedish citizen Gui Minhai was abducted in Thailand in 2015 and appeared later in a forced confession on Chinese state television. A Chinese court sentenced Gui to 10 years in prison for "illegally providing intelligence" to foreign governments. Before the sentence, the Chinese authorities claimed that his Chinese citizenship had been restored. According to Chinese law, he is no longer a Swedish citizen.

CHAPTER 17

CLAWS OF THE PANDA

For many decades China's communist leaders have quietly followed a policy of "soft power." They have carefully avoided actions or statements that would appear to be threatening to western nations. Meanwhile, they have quietly inserted spies, followers, and business leaders into North American society, in particular Canada, where former leaders such as Prime Minister Pierre Trudeau blindly and naively encouraged a growing relationship with the Dragon. It is only very recently that the gloves have come off and China shown its teeth to the world.

Given how far ahead the Chinese plan, this move from soft power to harsh action was likely discussed and implemented years ago, and it is only when leaders like Xi Jingping feel perfectly ready to attack western values that their behaviour changed. Many would argue that the Chinese leaders are correct in their bold assessment; it is far too late in the game for the western world to adapt. As its foreign policy, going ahead China will do whatever it wants to do. It can easily afford to do so.

The first exposé of this switch from soft to hard power is shown in renowned journalist Jonathan Manthorpe's brilliant 2019 book *Claws of the Panda*. As the book jacket notes explain, "Canada has continued to misjudge the reality of the relationship, while the Chinese Communist Party has benefited from Canadian naiveté." That's an understatement of the first order. Since 2019 the CCP has increased its bluster and issuing of threats and warnings to all western nations.

The synopsis on Amazon says *Claws of the Panda* tells the story of Canada's failure to construct a workable policy towards the People's Republic of China. In particular the book tells of Ottawa's failure to recognize and confront the efforts by the Chinese Communist Party to infiltrate and influence Canadian politics, academia, and media, and to exert control over Canadians of Chinese heritage. *Claws of the Panda* gives a detailed description of the CCP's campaign to embed agents of influence in Canadian business, politics, media and academia. The party's aims are to be able to turn Canadian public policy to China's advantage, to acquire useful technology and intellectual property, to influence Canada's international diplomacy, and, most important, to be able to monitor and intimidate Chinese Canadians and others it considers dissidents. The book traces the evolution of the Canada-China relationship over nearly 150 years. It shows how Canadian leaders have constantly misjudged the reality and potential of the relationship while the CCP and its agents have benefited from Canadian naiveté.

Blurbs from the back cover of the book go further. Hugh Segal, former Chair of the Foreign Affairs Committee of the Canadian Senate, states: "*Claws of the Panda* is a much-needed exposure of the CCP's step-by-step engagement through Canada and the world to advance its own economic, political, ideological, and strategic interests at the expense of other countries' sovereignty, security and economic well-being, if necessary." David Mulroney, former Canadian Ambassador to China, continues. "This is an important book for anyone who wants to understand China's growing influence in Canada."

Manthorpe sketches out the history. On page 100 he reveals where the nonsense started. Former Prime Minister Pierre Trudeau made his first trip to China in 1949, at the time of the establishment of the CCP regime. He criticized western countries for "refusing to recognize the existence of those who rule a quarter of the human race." He regarded it as "political and economic idiocy to fail to increase trading relations with the most formidable reservoir of consumption and production that ever existed."

Of course, this was back in 1949 before Mao reduced the surplus population of his country by tens of millions through his ill-planned Great Leap Forward initiative that starved many millions to death, and his in-

sane Cultural Revolution where students were urged to kill their teachers and teachers were forced to go work in the fields digging vegetables. But Trudeau's focus, even in 1949, was simply on profits that could be accrued by trading with the enemy, which the communists surely were even then. How was he to know that Chinese "production" would far outweigh its "consumption," at Canada's expense?

As Manthorpe continues, the senior Trudeau's words tend to support a criticism that was often levelled at him; his intellectualism blinded him to the emotions and subtleties that drive the political motives of other people. One can easily say "like father, like son." As Prime Minister, his son Justin Trudeau exhibited the same naiveté on trips to places like India, where the former drama teacher was heavily mocked for playing dress-up on his formal state visit, and for his initial support of increased trade with China, until research like Manthorpe's opened the eyes of the P.M. and many others. However, the lesson still has not been learned by many Canadians that the entire world is not a level playing field, and not everyone supports the quaint British belief in "fair play." Just wearing a western business suit and tie like Xi Jinping does not make a communist into a follower of democracy.

Who are the big time players in Canada that want to increase trade with communist china? On page 125 Manthorpe comes out and names them. The ten founding companies and financiers of the Canada-China Trade Council in 1978 were gold producer Barrack, BMO Financial, Bombardier, the China Trust and Investment Corporation, Export Development Canada, Manulife Financial, Power Corporation, Sun Life Financial, and SNC Lavalin. All were willing to look past human rights violations and the fact that their new partner was a communist nation, even though Canadians fought and died in Korea to stop the spread of communism.

Who else wants to do business with China? According to journalist Terry Glavin writing in *Maclean's* magazine in 2019, former Prime Minister Jean Chrétien "knows his way around the parasitical Communist Party elites that have lately decided to scuttle any of the institutions of the global order that would resist Beijing's efforts to reshape the world in its own image and likeness. Chrétien's 15 years of service to Chinese and Canadian corporations as a lobbyist, adviser, deal-maker, consultant and errand runner began officially only days after he resigned as Prime Minister after a decade in office in 2003."

According to the Embassy website for the People's Republic of China in Canada, the former PM was "an old friend." It states: "On February 13,

2001, President Jiang Zemin met with visiting Canadian Prime Minister Jean Chrétien at Zhongnanhai. Jiang first extended sincere congratulation to Chretien upon his re-election as Canadian Prime Minister and warmly welcomed his ongoing 4th visit to China. He noted that Chrétien is an old friend of China and expressed appreciation for his valuable contribution to the development of China-Canada relations. He added that the two have met on many bilateral and multilateral occasions in recent years. He recalled the warm reception accorded him by Chrétien during his visit to Canada in 1997, which is still fresh in his memory."

How many friends in high places do Huawei and the Chinese government have while pressuring Prime Minister Justin Trudeau's government for favourable treatment? Jean Charest, a former Quebec Liberal Premier and a former federal Progressive Conservative cabinet minister, has been working for Huawei as part of a legal team at McCarthy Tetrault. Charest joins a growing list of politicians and former politicians sympathetic to Huawei and China, or oblivious to the tense state of Canada-China relations. Prime Minister Trudeau had to fire former Liberal cabinet minister John McCallum as ambassador to China after McCallum backed the Chinese in the Huawai CEO legal team in her extradition case. According to the *Globe and Mail*, following his firing, McCallum, who has extensive business interests in China, told the *South China Morning Post* he urged the Chinese government through former contacts in its foreign affairs ministry "to play nice with Canada." How nice of him.

The last word goes to reporter Glavin, writing for the website *The Real Story*. "McCarthy Tétrault provides a variety of services to at least 20 Chinese corporate giants, including enterprises directly owned by the Chinese Communist Party regime in Beijing. Among those entities are Chinese banks currently engaged in a roaring money-lifeline trade with Russian enterprises in Moscow that have found themselves in a bit of bother with the NATO-member countries now that those doomsday financial sanctions have been kicking in after Vladimir Putin began his brutal war of conquest in Ukraine."

CHAPTER 18

WALMART AND THE DESTRUCTION
OF SMALL TOWN AMERICA

In his travel narrative *Deep South,* instead of exploring Africa or the Far East, renowned American travel writer Paul Theroux spends parts of several seasons touring the southern United States in his car, cruising through small towns ruined by the offshoring of jobs to China. On page 48 he summarizes his discovery. There was hardly any work, he wrote. There were no visitors, as in years past. Once there had been textile factories, making cloth and carpets. They'd closed, the manufacturing outsourced to China. There were some lumber mills, but they did not employ many people.

It was the same all over the South, in the ruined towns that had been manufacturing centers, sustained by the making of furniture, or appliances, or roofing materials, or plastic products, the labor-intensive jobs that kept a town ticking over. Companies had come to the South because the labor force was available and willing, wages were low, land was inexpensive, and unions were non-existent. Nowhere else in the United States could manufacturing be carried out so cheaply.

And that was the case until these manufacturers discovered that however cheap it was to make things in the right-to-work states of the South, it was even cheaper in sweatshop China. The contraction and impoverishment of the South had a great deal to do with the outsourcing of work to China and India. Even the catfish farms – an important income-producing industry all over the rural South – have been put out of business by the exports of fish farmers in Vietnam.

Theroux also detailed another reason why so many small towns had run to ruin. WalMart would build a regional store on the outskirts of town to avoid paying taxes. In time this would cripple all the mom and pop stores in town, whether pharmacies, hardware or sporting goods, whose owners would then be forced to work at Walmart for minimum wage. After destroying the town's economy, the WalMart itself might go out of business because no one had any money to shop at its superstore. Game over.

The history of Walmart began in 1950 when businessman Sam Walton purchased a store from Luther E. Harrison in Bentonville, Arkansas, and opened Walton's 5 & 10. Yes, a little Five and Dime was the beginning of the mighty Empire. The Walmart chain proper was founded in 1962 with a single store in Bentonville, expanding outside Arkansas by 1968 and throughout the rest of the southern United States by the 1980s, ultimately operating a store in every state of the United States, plus its first stores in Canada, by 1995. By the second decade of the 21st century, the chain had grown to over 11,000 stores in 27 countries.

Walton originally made the brilliant decision to achieve higher sales volumes by keeping sales prices lower than his competitors, often by reducing his profit margin. He understood that Americans "like a good deal." In fact, for many consumers, price is the only consideration. Walmart has destroyed tens of thousands of small businesses and countless manufacturing jobs over the past few decades. It has become a gigantic operation that sells five times more "stuff" than any other retailer in the United States. Unfortunately, a large percentage of the things sold at Walmart are made overseas. What that has cost the U.S. economy in lost jobs and revenue is incalculable.

In a time of want and poverty, one method of obtaining some small measure of happiness is to go buy some "stuff." It's easy to justify because the cost is low, and you are "getting a deal," and it's easy to ignore that what you are buying was made with sweatshop labor in a factory gulag in China.

Walmart's low-wage workers cost U.S. taxpayers billions of dollars in public assistance, including food stamps, Medicaid, and subsidized housing, according to a report published by the Americans for Tax Fairness, a coalition of 400 national and state-level groups. A 2013 study by the U.S. Committee on Education and the Workforce found that a single Walmart supercenter cost taxpayers between $904,542 and $1.75 million per year, or between $3,015 and $5,815 on average for each Walmart employee. That's because hundreds of thousands of full-time Walmart workers live below the poverty line and are forced to get state aid. Walmart has a long history of denying its employees the right to organize and the right to bargain collectively. The company deploys numerous anti-union tactics, including requiring workers to attend anti-union "captive-audience" meetings and training supervisors in "union avoidance."

In 2014, the company's largest shareholders, the Walton family, were known to be worth a combined total of $152 billion. The family's wealth now exceeds the wealth of the bottom 40 percent of American families combined, according to an analysis by the Economic Policy Institute. Yet Walmart's employees are among the lowest paid workers in the U.S. The vast majority of merchandise Walmart sells in the U.S. is manufactured abroad. The company searches the world for the cheapest goods possible, and this usually means buying from low-wage factories overseas. Walmart boasts of direct relationships with nearly 20,000 Chinese suppliers. According to the Economic Policy Institute, Walmart's trade with China alone eliminated 133,000 U.S. manufacturing jobs between 2001 and 2006 and accounted for 11.2 percent of the nation's total job loss due to trade.

Shopping? For many years I lived in a small two-bedroom Craftsman Cottage in North Vancouver. The little cottage came complete with white picket fence and a cherry tree in the back yard and radiated charm. Along with a dozen similar cottages on our street (known as Findlay's Row, after the developer) they were built just before the economic crash of 1912. The cottage did not have a hall closet to hang up coats or place any shoes. In those days people rich enough to buy a house (virtually anyone with a good job could do so) owned only two pairs of shoes, one for every day work and a second pair to go to church on Sunday. Today, according to a recent study by *ShopSmart* magazine, the average American woman owns 19 pairs of shoes, with 15 percent of women owning 30 or more pairs. Americans buy 7.5 pairs of new shoes each and every year.

According to fashion industry stats, the average Canadian household spends $285 on clothes per month. Manufacturing a pair of Levi's produces greenhouse gasses at the same rate as driving for 128 kilometres. *The Retail Insider* reveals that women's apparel was responsible for around 55 percent of total apparel sales in 2018. Furthermore, the 2018 growth was driven mainly by an increase in e-commerce and luxury apparel sales. Fashion industry statistics indicate that producing one basic cotton shirt requires 2,700 liters of water, the daily drinking needs of the average person for two and a half years. Additionally, global fashion industry statistics from 2020 showed that people worldwide use 5 trillion liters of water to dye fabric every year. According to a survey by Capsule Wardrobe Data, the average Canadian owns an average of 148 pieces of clothing, with most survey respondents owning between 77 to 155 pieces in their wardrobe with a few outliers in the 300-plus range. According to a survey of 1,000 American women, ClosetMaid found that the average woman has 103 items of clothing in her closet. The average American woman owns seven pairs of jeans, and men six pairs. Clothes thrown away account for a huge amount of waste in garbage dumps, according to a CBC Marketplace investigation. Canadians on average purchase 70 new articles of clothing a year and that contributes to the 12 million tons a year of textile waste dumped into North America's landfills.

A study published in the *Journal of Consumer Psychology* indicates that making purchases helps people feel instantly happier and also fights lingering sadness. One reason, the study authors speculate, is that making purchase decisions confers a sense of personal control and autonomy. Why do you feel happy after shopping? Dopamine is released even before a purchase is made. It's this simple anticipation of the eventual possibility of a reward or treat that releases dopamine, the hormone neurotransmitter in your brain that makes you feel good.

For some, this momentary pleasure can lead to compulsive shopping, as the instant reward and motivation to re-experience the "rush" starts to outweigh self-control and practical financial considerations. Compulsive spending is also known as oniomania, when a person feels an uncontrollable need to shop and spend, either for themselves or others. As the staggering increase in consumer spending attests, "retail therapy" (i.e. "shopping") is dramatically on the rise all over North America.

Sam Walton's three surviving children, Alice, Jim and Rob, daughter-in-law Christy and Christy's son, Lukas, own just under half the retailer,

Chongking is one of dozens of cities in China boasting luxury skyscrapers thanks to the wealth created by one-sided trade deals with the western world.

giving them a combined net worth of about $212 billion, according to the Bloomberg Billionaires Index. Doing the math, the Waltons make around $100 million per day from Walmart revenue. That's $70,000 per minute or $4 million per hour. The Walton Family Holdings Trust own over 50 percent of Walmart's total shares, or over $3 billion just in dividends each year. Not only are they the wealthiest family in America, but they top the charts as the richest family in the world.

Then there is the Rust Belt. According to the website Investopedia, the term is often used in a derogatory sense to describe parts of the country that have seen a typically drastic economic decline. The Rust Belt region represents the de-industrialization of an area, which is often accompanied by fewer high-paying jobs and high poverty rates. The result has been a change in the urban landscape as the local population moves to other areas of the country in search of work. It often refers to specific, formerly-prosperous manufacturing centers in Midwestern and Northeastern cities like Detroit and Toledo, Ohio, Pittsburgh, and Buffalo, New York.

Blue-collar jobs have increasingly moved overseas, forcing local governments to re-think the type of manufacturing businesses that can succeed in the area. While some cities managed to adopt new technologies, others still struggle with rising poverty levels and declining populations. In 2020 the unemployment rate in West Virginia was 14 percent; in Ohio 12.5 percent.

Before being known as the Rust Belt, the area was generally known as the country's Manufacturing Belt. This area, once a booming hub of economic activity, represented a great portion of U.S. industrial growth and development. Most research suggests that the Rust Belt started to falter in the late 1970s. The Rust Belt is still mostly dominated by older, non-college-educated white voters, which traditionally lean toward the Republican Party.

Once prosperous American cities from Detroit to Buffalo to Pittsburgh have turned into economic wastelands, with shuttered factories and empty houses. Meanwhile, glistening steel and glass towers pop up in China using the wealth derived from consumers in the Western world searching for cheap sources of happiness, "looking for love in all the wrong places." Perhaps, if they are willing to work real cheap, they could move to China.

HOW THE U.S. OLIGARCHY BUILT AND MAINTAINS ITS WEALTH

Robert Reich, a former US secretary of labor, is professor of public policy at the University of California at Berkeley. Writing in the *Guardian*, he reports that the theft of money from the American middle class started four decades ago. According to a recent RAND study, he said, if America's distribution of income had remained the same as it was in the three decades following the Second World War, the bottom 90 percent would now be $47 trillion richer.

A low-income American earning $35,000 this year would be earning $61,000. A college-educated worker now earning $72,000 would be earning $120,000. Overall, the grotesque surge in inequality that began 40 years ago is costing the median American worker $42,000 per year. The upward redistribution of $47 trillion wasn't due to natural forces. It was contrived. As wealth accumulated at the top, so did political power to siphon off even more wealth and shaft everyone else.

Monopolies expanded because anti-trust laws were neutered. Labor unions shriveled because corporations were allowed to bust unions. Wall Street was permitted to gamble with other people's money and was bailed out when its bets soured even as millions lost their homes and savings. Taxes on the top were cut, tax loopholes widened.

When COVID-19 hit, big tech cornered the market, the rich traded on inside information and the Treasury and the Fed bailed out big corporations but let small businesses go under. Billionaire wealth has soared while most of America has become poorer. How could the oligarchy get away with this in a democracy where the bottom 90 percent have the votes? Because the bottom 90 percent are bitterly divided.

Long before Trump, the GOP suggested to white working-class voters that their real enemies were Black people, Latinos, immigrants, "coastal elites," bureaucrats and "socialists." Trump rode their anger and frustration into the White House with more explicit and incendiary messages. After losing the White house he kept going with his bonkers claim of a stolen election.

The oligarchy surely appreciates the Trump-GOP tax cuts, regulatory rollbacks and the most business-friendly Supreme Court since the early 1930s. But the Trump-GOP's biggest gift has been an electorate more fiercely split than ever. Into this melee comes Joe Biden, who speaks of being "president of all Americans" and collaborating with the Republican Party. But the GOP doesn't want to collaborate. When Biden holds out an olive branch, Mitch McConnell and other Republican leaders respond just as they did to Barack Obama, with more warfare, because that maintains their power and keeps the big money rolling in.

Chapter 19

Toronto the Big

Capitalism is against the things that we say we believe in – democracy, freedom of choice, fairness. It's not about any of those things now. It's about protecting the wealthy

– Michael Moore

The view from the top of the CN Tower in downtown Toronto is quite something, and well worth the long line-up to see it, but as a guest of the Tourism Board I am given preferential treatment and up I go with no waiting. I find the elevator is not quite as fast as Taipei 101 in Taiwan or the Barg Khalifa in Dubai, but on a clear day from the top of the tower you can see all across Lake Ontario, plus you get a bird's eye view of the rest of the Toronto downtown area which has evolved into quite a sight.

When I first came to Toronto in the late 1960's "Toronto the Good" had a reputation for blandness. Growing up in Montreal in my day, nobody ever went to Toronto. Instead, Torontonians came to Montreal, to party. You couldn't get a beer on Sundays in Toronto, and when the liquor store was open you had to fill in papers to buy beer and it was deliberately kept warm. In those days, the only good thing about Toronto was their hockey team. Not anymore.

My first impression upon arriving and setting foot on a bustling sidewalk was that Toronto must be the most multicultural city in the world. I heard Spanish, Greek, Italian and other accents I couldn't place. Foot traffic in TO moves twice the speed I normally walk. These are people on their way somewhere important. Lucky for me I had reservations at the Chelsea Hotel, at 1,500 rooms the largest hotel in Canada. From this central headquarters I could walk anywhere, and I did, first north to the Royal Ontario Museum. I found Yorkville, once a hippie hangout, is now fully upscale. A quick walk east to Church and Wellesley, aka the Gay Village. South down Yonge Street to Dundas Square to watch the street performers. The old Maple Leaf Gardens, now a Loblaws grocery store.

The next day a stroll around Old Town, and the organized chaos that is St. Lawrence Market, then the new Distillery District, brought back from the dead by cobblestones and ingenuity, people-watching at its prime. I discovered that the baseball stadium (Skydome), hockey rink, entertainment District (CN Tower, bars and clubs) were also all within walking distance of my hotel. So were Chinatown (murals and restaurants) and the wonderful funky haze of outdoor Kensington Market, the Haight-Ashbury of Canada. Who said the sixties are dead? The Frank Gehry-designed Art Gallery of Ontario was hosting a Lawren Harris exhibition. All within ambling distance of my hotel.

Little Portugal, Koreatown, Little Italy, Little India, Little Malta; I learned there are 240 official and unofficial neighborhoods within the city's boundaries. The former city of small villages has finally morphed into one gargantuan metropolis, nearly six million people with hundreds of cultures. As the CCP impose sweeping security laws in Hong Kong, residents of that city continue to move tens of billions of dollars across the globe to places in Canada like Toronto. Capital flows out of Hong Kong banks reaching Canada have risen to their highest levels on record in electronic funds transfers (EFT) recorded by FINTRAC, Canada's anti-money laundering agency, which receives reports on transfers above $10,000 Cdn. At the same time, the FINTRAC data captures only a fraction of total legal inflows into the Canadian economy because many transactions are not included, such as transfers via cryptocurrencies, between financial institutions, or under $10,000 Cdn.

According to an article in *Maclean's* magazine, the original amphetamine rush of Chinese cash has been felt far beyond Vancouver and the Fraser Valley in British Columbia with a large percentage of new condominiums being built in central Toronto now going to foreign buyers, according to a survey by the Canada Mortgage and Housing Corporation (CMHC); real estate market experts believe the vast majority are mainland Chinese. On Juwai.com, an online listing service where Chinese buyers can look for international real estate, inquiries about specific properties in Ontario rose 143 per cent as early as 2015, with the total value of those homes hitting $11.2 billion.

Next to China's own volatile real estate markets, property almost anywhere in the Western world can seem an island of financial sanity. According to Juwai.com, the year-on-year property value increase in Shenzhen, one of China's tier-one cities across the bay from Hong Kong, is close to 60 per cent. Even the most privileged Chinese mainlanders have for

Overseas (i.e. Chinese) investment in Toronto has created a huge rise in the cost of living, with Canadian citizens unable to compete with the wealth of Chinese investors.

decades been shut out of buying property, the favorite asset class of the Chinese dating back to its pre-Revolution days. This is on top of profound worries many Chinese have about their country's overbearing political system, the lack of transparent rule of law and rampant corruption.

In Canada, the actions of the CCP are driving house values out of reach for even well-off professionals, while raising the risk of a crash at the first sign of adverse conditions. Yet the self-same conditions are adding to the net worth of millions of Canadian homeowners, and supporting many housing-related industries from real estate sales to interior decoration. The question going forward isn't so much what Chinese buyers are doing to the Canadian property market; it's what might happen without them.

Estimates peg the amount Chinese investors and companies move out of that country each year at nearly $1 trillion. As early as 2014 there were 3.6 million millionaires in China, many desperately seeking safer places to invest their money. Most put foreign real estate at the top of their list. In Canada, everything in your bank account is your own, as long as you pay taxes. In China, even if the government's name is not on your account, whenever they want your money they will take your money.

Strolling around among the hullabaloo, watching Toronto explode and expand into an international colossus, I am pleased to remind myself that

Vancouver has not yet reached these dimensions. Then again, I am saddened to remind myself that – just like the CN Tower – the "sky is the limit," and many people plan for Vancouver to grow just as big. It makes me wonder why.

"Growth for the sake of growth is the ideology of the cancer cell," wrote environmentalist Edward Abbey in 1976. He was referring to the ever-diminishing wild places of his beloved Arizona, replaced by sprawling subdivisions that housed a ballooning population of retirees, alongside massive mining and oil operations run by multinationals. When Abbey's essay "The Blob Comes To Arizona" was written in 1976, Arizona was the fastest growing state in the Union. Out of concern for the impact such a rapid rate of growth was having on the ecology of the high desert, Abbey sought some answers from the governor at the time, Raul Castro.

"I tried to pin the Governor down on the question of just how much growth is good and how much is too much? At what point, I wanted to know, should we in Arizona draw the line? The Governor would not be pinned. Dismissing the question as hypothetical – and of course it is hypothetical, that's why I asked it – he went on with other matters."

At present the federal government of Canada has decided to encourage immigration to our country to the tune of around 400,000 people per year, which works out to over a million new residents every three years. One needs to trust the government that this is a wise policy to adopt. However, it does make one wonder where all these new immigrants will be coming from. At the present rate of immigration from China, eventually the Chinese will form a majority in some communities. Of course, just bringing up the topic brands one as a racist, so best we not go down that path. I wander down Yonge Street back to my hotel and note that the line-up to check in to the hotel is all across the lobby and out the door, perhaps not surprising when there are 1,500 rooms. Toronto the Good has been transformed into Toronto the Big, and who knows whether that is a good thing or not?

CANADIAN CEOS GET EVEN RICHER

In 2020, as many Canadians had hours cut or lost their jobs completely during repeated pandemic lockdowns and forced closures, the highest-paid 100 CEOs at publicly traded companies earned an average of $10.9 million. That was down from the record high of $11.8 million in 2018, but an increase of $95,000 compared with 2019.

David Macdonald, a senior economist at The Canadian Centre for Policy Alternatives, said that CEOs receiving the second-highest pay on record is "quite an achievement" given that the pandemic was damaging to many of the companies they were running. More than 82 per cent of the average income came through bonuses including cash or stock options, which Macdonald said companies creatively calculated to ensure poor performance during the pandemic didn't affect CEO pay.

"This only happens in bad times," said Macdonald. "When things go badly for the company, CEOs are protected in many cases. When things go well for the company, the sky's the limit. It really illustrates the bankruptcy of the idea that this is somehow based on merit."

Macdonald said CEOs often justify their bonuses with claims the bonuses are only paid because they are exceptional at their jobs, but he said half the CEOs who got bonuses in 2020, worked at companies which received government aid like the Canada Emergency Wage Subsidy or only received the bonus because of an adjustment to the bonus formula. The top-paid CEOs made 191 times more than the average worker in 2020, which was down from 202 times as much in 2019, and the lowest gap between the CEOs and average workers in six years. Macdonald recommended the federal government create a wealth tax for the richest Canadians, as the wide gap between the average income of Canadians and the highest-paid CEOs is set to broaden further over time.

A typical Taiwanese transport
Photo courtesy pxfuel

CHAPTER 20

TAIWAN AND THE BEAR

The richest one percent of this country owns half our country's wealth, five trillion dollars. You got ninety percent of the American public out there with little or no net worth. Now you're not naive enough to think we're living in a democracy, are you buddy? It's the free market, and you're a part of it. Greed, for lack of a better word, is good. Greed is right. Greed works. Greed clarifies, cuts through, and captures the essence of the evolutionary spirit. Greed, in all of its forms, greed for life, for money, for love, knowledge, has marked the upward surge in mankind.
　　　　　　　- Gordon Gekko, in the movie *Wall Street*

On my first trip to Taiwan years ago, courtesy Taiwan Tourism, I went with a photographer who shall be called Brian, because he doesn't deserve the courtesy of having his full name mentioned. The agreement with Taiwan Tourism was that I would write an article about Taiwan for Canadian newspapers. I did. In fact, I liked Taiwan so much I wrote and published several articles about Taiwan, the first titled "All of China in One Small Island." The title is self-explanatory. Brian, a professional photographer, took thousands of photos and shot lots of video footage, with the understanding that he would produce a documentary. He never did.

There is so much to absorb in Taiwan. "All of China" could refer just to the food. There are eight major cuisines in China; Anhui, Cantonese, Fujian, Hunan, Jiangsu, Shandong, Szechuan and Zhejiang. They are all available in Taiwan. Should that not prove of interest there is American-style Chinese food like General Tso's chicken, egg rolls, wonton soup, fried rice and sweet and sour dishes. In the bigger cities like Taipei and Taichung you can find pizza, hamburgers, KFC and other western food. Taiwan is very cosmopolitan and sophisticated.

We were in Hualien, in eastern Taiwan at the airport, waiting for a plane, when out of boredom Brian started to shoot photos of the jets, especially the Air Force planes. He was standing right next to a sign warning that the airport was also a military base and that photos were strictly forbidden and subject to criminal penalties. Given that being arrested would cause severe embarrassment to Taiwan Tourism, I pointed out the sign to Brian.

"Who cares?" he said, snapping away. "What are they going to do? Arrest us?"

Yes, I thought, the Taiwanese are very polite, and it's unlikely they will slap handcuffs on us, but perhaps we Canadians should also be polite and respect their regulations. Also, the Taiwanese stand on guard against an attack and invasion by the Chinese military, and have every right to be concerned about security. At that time, I didn't know exactly how dangerous that military threat really was, but it came in sharp focus later.

Years later on my fifth and final tour of the island, always courtesy of the courteous Taiwan Tourism Bureau, I hired a professional cinematographer named James, about whom I will say little except that he also broke his contract and never produced the documentary we had promised. James was obviously a talented videographer, judging by the footage he showed me at our hotels every night after dinner on our tour. Sadly, he shared the same disrespect as Brian did to the very polite Taiwanese people we met, seemingly incapable of matching their excellent manners.

We were at the station just south of Taipei where passengers could buy tickets to board the so-called "Bullet Train," the high-speed rail that runs down the west coast of the island all the way to Kaohsiung in the south, reaching speeds in excess of 300 kph. In the spirit of the character I had created as an "Innocent Tourist" for the documentary, I made some jokes at the ticket counter about wanting to buy a ticket to New York City, and is it called the Bullet Train because people shoot at it? Silly stuff, and so on.

Encouraged by the silly bravado I had just shown, James started to shoot video footage of the train platform, passengers walking by, and the sort of "B Roll" (background footage) necessary for any documentary. I was standing next to a sign that read "No Video allowed" when we spotted two transit police hustling our way, pointing at us to stop. I indicated to James that he should stop filming and put his camera away, but he simply grinned and kept shooting. He even kept the camera rolling when the police arrived and pointed at him to stop.

"What the hell are you doing?" I asked through gritted teeth, as the police politely explained to me the rules and regulations, in good English, before walking away.

The towering Taipei 101 skyscraper stands in the centre of the capital city of Taiwan, a freedom-loving democracy across the sea from its communist enemy Mainland China.

"I was hoping you would get arrested," he said, putting away his camera. "It would be great for the documentary." There is an asshole lurking around every corner, I thought, but mocking the police is not a laughing matter.

When Mao (CCP) beat Chiang Kai-shek (ROC) for the right to rule China back in the day, the Kuomintang subsequently beat a hasty retreat over to the island of Formosa, now known as Taiwan. Joining the KMT were many business people, creative people, intelligentsia, artists and others who realized that life under communism might not be in their best interests. It is an over-simplification to say that the "best and brightest of the Chinese" fled the mainland, but there is some truth to that. Over the years the two societies have gone totally different directions. The mainland remains a strict communist society, and after some twists and turns along the way Taiwan has become a democratic country based on western capitalism. The two countries are complete opposites.

After fleeing the premises for safer if not greener pastures, General Chiang Kai-shek repeatedly stated that "there is only one China," and that he was the boss of the real China, holding fort just a hop, skip and jump away on a nearby island and only on a temporary basis. Supported by the American military, he could afford to maintain this pretense, but the reality was the General was never going to re-capture the leadership. Stating there was "only one China" allowed Chairman Mao to agree with his adversary, and to attack Formosa in order to re-attach the runaway province

161

back to the mainland. This reckless boast by Kai-Shek has proved disastrous in the long run for Taiwan, allowing subsequent Chinese mainland leaders to this day to insist that there is only one China, even though the Communists had never set foot in Formosa so "taking it back" is not a choice for them to make.

Every tourist to Taiwan must go to the National Museum in Taipei. According to my friends at Wikipedia, the National Palace Museum, originally established in 1925 in Beijing, has a permanent collection of nearly 700,000 pieces of Chinese artifacts and artworks, many of which were "moved" (i.e. "removed") from the original Palace Museum in Beijing, as well as five other institutions throughout mainland China during the ROC retreat, making the museum in Taipei one of the largest museums of its type in the world. The museum's collection encompasses items spanning 8,000 years of Chinese history from the neo-lithic age to the modern period. Most of the collection is high quality pieces collected by Chinese Emperors, taken from mainland China. Little of the art in the museum in Taipei is actually from Taiwan.

During the 1960s and 1970s, the National Palace Museum was used by the Kuomintang to support its claim that the ROC was the sole legitimate government of all China, because it was the sole preserver of traditional Chinese culture amid the social chaos and devastation during the Cultural Revolution in mainland China, so the Museum wouldn't otherwise exist.

The sharp-eyed observer will note that the Museum's collection started many years ago back in Beijing. The long history of China now resides offshore, where affluent mainland Chinese tourists can visit their own history and wonder why it is residing in another country. This presents both a huge problem and huge opportunity for Taiwan that can easily be resolved by the Taiwan government offering an olive branch and returning the 700,000 artifacts to Beijing, along with a "sorry, I forgot, this is yours" apology. This would certainly produce something of a dent in the Taiwan tourism industry, but might prove cheaper in the long run for the ROC than attempting to battle the PLA (People's Liberation Army), now poised to invade at the earliest possible provocation, and to take back their artwork along with seizing the invaluable high-tech economic prize that Taiwan currently presents.

Never mind returning stolen artifacts to their owner, there is the more urgent issue of an invasion being threatened by the CCP. Given what Russia has done to its neighbors, including the invasion of Ukraine, many people are starting to pay attention to the vast Chinese military and its increasing threats to attack Taiwan. I have published several OpEds about this topic in the *Vancouver Sun,* and spoken with various Director-Generals at the Taipei Economic and Cultural Office in Vancouver (which acts as an unofficial embassy) and today I am off to meet with Andy Chen, the current Director-General.

I am interested in returning a sixth time to Taiwan, I explain to Andy, but the problem is I have "been there, done that" and the only region I haven't explored in Taiwan is the high mountains that run down the centre of the island. Chatting on the topic, I soon learn that there is a creature in Taiwan somewhat akin to the ghostly "spirit bear" of the Great Bear Rainforest in British Columbia. I spent quite some time tracking down the spirit bear and shooting photos and video of the creature, before it became known to the public as a symbol of the forest. I am keen to find another bear that represents freedom.

The Taiwanese black bear is an extremely rare and secretive creature that was thought to be extinct in Taiwan but has lately been spotted. Nothing like a steep hike in high mountains to search for rare creatures, I think, so Andy and I discuss the possibility. Andy produces a small ceramic bear with a black coat and white throat and hands it to me as a gift. The Formosan black bear, also known as the Taiwanese white-throated bear, is a subspecies of the Asiatic black bear. They live only in the high mountains and are seldom seen. They have been on the Endangered Species list since 1989. The government of Taiwan has made the decision to put images of the white-throated bear on government stationary to act as a symbol of the country. It's not as cute as a panda, I say, but thank you for the gift. I will keep it on my shelf next to the computer.

Ah, the panda! says Andy. China has successfully used the panda as a national symbol for decades, he says. It's cute, peaceful and cuddly and serves as a useful promotional tool so the CCP can say that China is not a threat to anyone. Have you ever seen what they do to other bears in China? he asks. It's a disgrace and a true representation of the way the people on the mainland are ignorant and don't care about the pain and suffering their actions might occur. So I do some research on bears in China. What I find is horrible.

According to *National Geographic Magazine,* bear bile has been used in traditional Chinese medicine for thousands of years, with the first reference appearing in an eighth century medical text prescribing bear bile for maladies like epilepsy, hemorrhoids, and heart pain. In the early 1900s, scientists discovered that bear bile, a fluid that's secreted by the liver and

Tens of thousands of black bears are kept locked in cages in China while their gall bladders are drained every day to provide folk medicine.
Photo courtesy of Pixabay

stored in the gallbladder, contains a significant amount of ursodeoxycholic acid - more than other animals like pigs or cows. This acid is medically proven to help dissolve gallstones and treat liver disease.

Bear bile, however, is also marketed as a cure for cancer, colds, hangovers, and more, though there is no scientific evidence whatsoever supporting its effectiveness for these ailments. It's also sometimes used as an ingredient in household products like toothpaste, acne treatment, tea, and shampoo as a way to expand the market for bear bile beyond traditional medicine, according to Animals Asia.

Meanwhile Wikipedia explains that the "bile bears," sometimes called "battery bears," are kept in tiny cages to harvest their bile. It is estimated that 12,000 bears are farmed for bile in China and Southeast Asia. The species most commonly farmed for bile is the Asiatic black bear, although the sun bear, brown bear and every other species are also used (the only exception being the giant panda). They are listed as "vulnerable" on the Red List of Threatened Animals. They were previously hunted for bile in the wild but factory farming has become common since hunting was banned in the 1980s. The bile can be harvested using several techniques, all of which require some degree of surgery. A significant proportion of the bears die because of the stress of unskilled surgery or the infections which occur.

Farmed bile bears are housed continuously in small cages which often prevent them from standing or sitting upright, or from turning around. These highly restrictive cage systems cause severe mental stress and muscle atrophy. Some bears are caught as cubs and may be kept in these conditions for up to 30 years. The value of the bear products trade is estimated as high as $2 billion. The practice of factory farming bears for bile has been extensively condemned, including by Chinese physicians.

The conversation turns away from bears to the future of Taiwan, and the threat of invasion. Andy produces a giant hand-drawn map he has made himself, showing Taiwan's location in the South China Sea and explains why the island's location is so important as a military base. The Spanish and Japanese occupied the island before, but China has big plans for its little neighbor. The CCP has started building military bases on sandbars on the South China Sea created by their PLA troops, landing strips for their planes. The CCP have serious plans to expand their territory eastward, says Andy, and control the Pacific Ocean. Little Taiwan stands in the immediate way and must be seized in one way or another.

Indeed, the CCP are now making vague noises about the South China Sea "not really being in international waters," open to shipping by all nations, but strictly a territory belonging only to China. American warships and other vessels from other nations have been told to stop cruising through the straits. The U.S. government, under the administration of former President Obama years ago, quietly made a shift in global policy and started to focus on Asia, and specifically the South China Sea, and subsequent American governments have now made the region a global priority. Taiwan sits right smack dab in the middle of the action.

It pays to be a CEO in the U.S.

The ratio between CEO and average worker pay

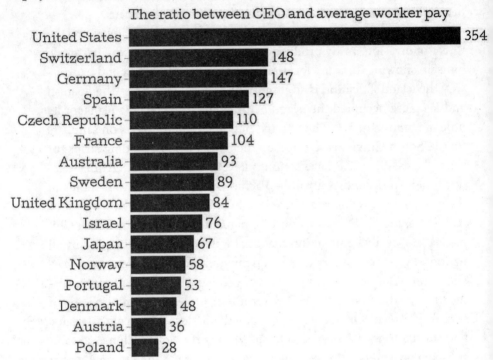

United States	354
Switzerland	148
Germany	147
Spain	127
Czech Republic	110
France	104
Australia	93
Sweden	89
United Kingdom	84
Israel	76
Japan	67
Norway	58
Portugal	53
Denmark	48
Austria	36
Poland	28

Made with Chartbuilder

Data: How Much (More) Should CEOs Ma

THE FINAL WORD

Political satire became obsolete when Henry Kissinger was awarded the Nobel Peace Prize.

> – Tom Lehrer

In a December 26, 2016 OpEd column I published in the *Vancouver Sun* (one of about 40 OpEds I published in the *Sun* on various topics) about the reality of "offshoring jobs to China," I wrote the following:

> According to the Economic Policy Institute, CEOs of America's largest corporations now earn 10 times more than 30 years ago. The growth of CEO and executive compensation overall is a major factor in doubling the income of the top one percent of U.S. households. Average annual CEO compensation for top executives of large corporations is now up to $16.3 million. From 1978 to 2014, inflation-adjusted CEO compensation has increased 997 percent contrasted with the 10.9 percent growth in a typical worker's annual compensation. (*Update: Yes, the increase in corporate executive pay differs greatly in different chapters of this book, depending on the source, many of which also report an overall annual 10 percent decline in workers compensation in the past 30 years.*)
>
> That CEO income grew far faster than pay of the top 0.1 percent of wage earners indicates that CEO compensation growth does not simply reflect the increased value of highly paid professionals in a competitive race for skills (the "market for talent"), meaning CEO compensation does not reflect greater productivity of executives but rather the power of CEOs to extract concessions. Consequently, if CEOs earned less or were taxed more, there would be no adverse impact on output or employment.

That OpEd was then, this is now. Offshoring has been spectacularly successful for the western executives who designed and executed the plan, as well as the Communist cadres who agreed to cooperate and assisted in its implementation. Not so lucky have been the ordinary citizens in the western world whose place in "globalization" is now as a simple-minded consumer of cheaply manufactured goods. Trillions of consumer dollars have gone to China, while cheap manufactured goods end up in the endlessly growing landfills of the west in return. Here in Vancouver, we can't even find a new place to bury our garbage.

Western consumers have become addicted to consumerism as a substitute for happiness. Drug addicts have become simply death statistics thanks to the Chinese manufacturing and export of fentanyl that has killed more people than Covid. There is no cure for either product. It is impossible for Canadian and American exporters of raw materials to pull the plug on their relationship with China. The two economies are too closely tied together. Big corporations in Canada have too much power over the Canadian government, their financial support keeping the politicians in office.

While there seems to be no light on the horizon, thanks to technology these days the world changes at lightning speed. In the cosmic scope of things, and also in Chinese history, 1971 is like yesterday, just a blink of the eye. It's impossible to predict the future, but for sure ongoing change is guaranteed. It depends on what kind of change. Thanks to global warming, we cannot continue to do business the way we have done in the past few hundred years. We cannot continue to cut down all the trees, dig great big holes in the ground, pollute the oceans, eat all the fish, and foul the air. If we do the planet will exact its revenge and the human race will disappear.

There is an enormous cost to extracting raw resources to produce unnecessary consumer goods. Just the amount of water needed to create a pair of blue jeans is incredible. We cannot continue to make material goods to throw them away and buy more. The damage already done to the planet is mindboggling. Huge floods sweep many countries, some of which will soon disappear because they will be permanently under water. Savage storms, typhoons and hurricanes destroy vast amounts of property. Searing heat and drought means that many people cannot continue to live where they are and must move. Where will they go? As the old slave song says: "A change is gonna come." Or, as a more modern folk song attests: "The times they are a changing." But which way?

It can be argued that the criminal President Nixon was aware of the Marshall Plan, a brilliant blueprint written by Secretary of State George Marshall, who in 1947 proposed that the United States provide economic assistance to restore the economic infrastructure of postwar Europe. This allowed Japan and Germany to rise from the ashes of World War II – a conflict they started in the first place with their thirst for ethnic and economic global domination – when Nixon proposed to make peace with the Chinese communists. It can be more easily argued that he wished to change his reputation from an ethically challenged political whore to a "global statesman," which also served to divert attention from his various crimes like Watergate.

It cannot be proved that Nixon knew that creating a partnership with the enemy communist China, which eventually has evolved into what is now known as "globalization," would result in the termination of tens of millions of good paying American jobs. However, as a Far Right Wing politician it is doubtful Tricky Dick would care anything about what happened to ordinary blue collar working people whose lives would be ruined altogether. Nixon's thinking remains the same as among current Far Right supporters. Life is hard, they say. The world is full of bad people. All that matters is winning. To the victor go the spoils. Whatever.

That direction points to the abyss. Thankfully Mother Nature has some things to say as well. If we wish to continue to stay alive as human beings on Planet Earth, we need to change our shabby and self-serving ways. "He who sups with the Devil should have a long spoon" is a medieval idiom that William Shakespeare refers to twice in his plays. It's time to sever the greasy connection with the enemy and move forward. There is more to life than cheap and expedient profit, or a new pair of shoes, and true happiness comes from knowing that what you are doing is good for everyone. The planet will thank you for it.

Michael McCarthy
Vancouver, 2023

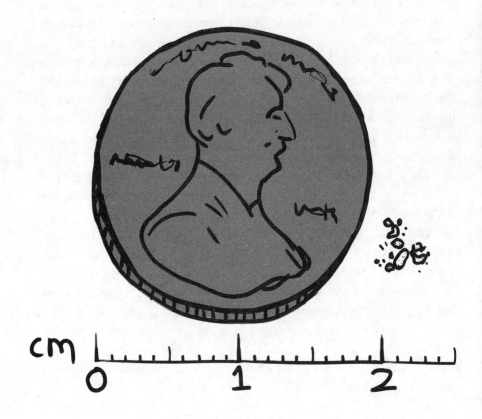

Lethal Dose of Fentanyl
Creative Commons, Eldridge Misnomer

APPENDIX

FENTANYL

CANADA

According to the Public Safety Canada 2018 Law Enforcement Roundtable on the Opioid Crisis, China has been identified as the main source country of fentanyl found in Canada. In the Dominican Republic, police investigations in laboratories revealed that pill presses were being used. In Mexico, precursors were found during searches, suggesting that fentanyl is also being synthesized in that country. Domestically, laboratories producing fentanyl have been found in British Columbia, Alberta, and Quebec by those with expertise in chemistry related to methamphetamines and are transferring their knowledge to develop fentanyl.

While some organized crime groups are dealing fentanyl, large cartels do not play a major role. Cartels and organized crime operations have large supply chains and distribution networks because they need to sell large quantities of the substances to turn a profit. The logistics of importing and distributing such high volumes mean that only a few groups are able to take on this role.

Because of its potency, fentanyl is moved using other methods. Small amounts of fentanyl can be imported and then cut into other drugs to increase volume. Fentanyl is also easily obtained from the dark web and transported through the regular mail service. Typically, fentanyl traffickers use the drug themselves or are mid- to low-level traffickers. Rather than being involved in the distribution chain, traditional organized crime groups may be involved in violent intimidation and taxing of those who are dealing opioids.

The Canadian Centre on Drug Abuse reports that fentanyl analogues made in clandestine laboratories can be significantly more toxic than pharmaceutical-grade fentanyl. Therefore, individuals who are using heroin, Oxycontin or other substances, but mistakenly take fentanyl, are at greater risk of an accidental overdose. *A Globe and Mail* article states that labs in China tailor custom variations of fentanyl. The labs manufacture the main ingredient used in the production of fentanyl, as well as analogues – drugs that have chemical structures differing only slightly from the pharmaceutical-grade version. One of the best-known fentanyl analogues is alpha-methylfentanyl, known on the streets as China White.

Distributors sell the drug online, with delivery guaranteed. On forums such as EC21 and WeiKu, transactions are conducted in English. The websites are available to anyone and signing up for an account takes minutes. The sites guarantee delivery and ask customers only for a shipping address and credit-card number.

Before it is shipped, the drug is hidden in a decoy package. Suppliers in China often conceal the fentanyl powder in silica packages placed alongside a pack of urine test strips. Another way is to gift-wrap the package or label it as household detergent with an accompanying certificate of analysis. *The Canada Border Services Agency* inspects goods coming into the country through the mail system and by courier, but the agency is authorized to open only those packages weighing more than 30 grams and needs the supplier's permission to open smaller ones. Larger quantities do arrive hidden in cargo shipments, including farm machinery and car parts. To dilute the drug, the labs cut it with powdered sugar, baby powder or antihistamines. They also mix it into other drugs, such as heroin, or pack it into pills which are often made to look like OxyContin: dyed green and stamped with an "80" – the oxy dosage. A kilogram of pure fentanyl powder costs $12,500. A kilo is enough to make 1 million tablets. Each tab sells for $20 in major cities, for total proceeds of $20-million. In smaller markets, the street price is as high as $80.

A *Global TV* report reveals that Canada turned down China's request to insert a new police liaison officer in China's Vancouver consulate. "If you anger the Chinese they won't work with you," said the *Global TV* source. "The fentanyl coming into Canada is going to get worse. Nothing will happen because we have to satisfy what they (the Chinese government) want." China's request to send a police liaison to Vancouver was rejected by Canada's department of Global Affairs because of national security concerns, according to their source. The concern is the police liaison could have worked for China's Ministry of State Security, which is the non-military agency responsible for China's counter-intelligence, foreign intelligence and political security operations.

What China wants, said the report, is freedom in B.C. to pursue alleged corruption suspects and financial fugitives, including a suspect accused of absconding with about $1 billion from a Beijing company. The suspect is laundering the money in Vancouver real estate, a source said, and using Vancouver as a hub to launder dirty money around the world.

Another *Global News* investigation has found that in British Columbia, where the crisis has hit hardest, investigators believe the fentanyl trade revolves around the Big Circle Boys, a powerful crime network directed from the Chinese mainland, with an ability to corrupt Chinese officials, which allows them to control chemical factories in southern China and get fentanyl through Chinese customs and to the West. "There are so many players we identified in B.C. But this is all directed from inside China," an international policing expert said. "At the very top they are insulated. It's government officials."

MEXICO

According to a report from *Reuters*, in April 2023 Mexico's president said he had written to his Chinese counterpart Xi Jinping, urging him to help control shipments of fentanyl. President Lopez Obrador defended efforts to curb supply of the deadly drug, while rounding on U.S. critics, some of whom want Washington to intervene militarily in Mexico. Lopez Obrador says fentanyl laboratories have sprung up in Mexico, and he told Xi that law enforcement had last year destroyed nearly 1,400 clandestine labs mixing the drug with other substances, and seized seven tons of it. Lopez Obrador says Mexico does not produce fentanyl and that cartels buy it direct from Asia. He said that only 30 percent of the drug consumed in the U.S. enters via Mexico. U.S. officials contest that view, arguing the opioid is mass-produced in the country using chemicals sourced largely from China.

Most fentanyl in the United States is smuggled across the southern border, U.S. officials say. Although fentanyl coming directly from China – previously the dominant source – has significantly decreased since 2019, experts note that many drug shipments from China are merely being re-routed through Mexico. Mexican cartels will "almost certainly have the greatest direct impact" on the U.S. fentanyl market in the coming years, the DEA cautions. Since 2007, the United States has provided Mexico with more than $3 billion in security and counter-narcotics aid, including for police and judicial reforms, in a program known as the Merida Initiative. The DEA has also coordinated efforts with China, the primary source of fentanyl in the United States. Amid sustained U.S. diplomatic pressure, Beijing made several moves to crack down on fentanyl production, culminating in a 2019 ban on the production, sale, and export of all fentanyl-related substances. Experts note, however, that Beijing's cooperation has lessened as bilateral relations have strained.

The *Justice Department* has ramped up efforts to prosecute those involved in overprescribing and trafficking. In 2018, it partnered with nearly all state attorneys general to share opioid prescription information in order to investigate drug crimes and soon after brought charges against more than 150 doctors, nurses, pharmacists, and others for their alleged roles in distributing opioids. Two years later, the department filed a civil suit against Walmart for allegedly failing to stop hundreds of thousands of improper prescriptions.

USA

Before the COVID health crisis, the skyrocketing increase in fentanyl-related overdose deaths in America was mainly affecting the eastern half of the U.S., and hit especially hard in urban areas like Washington, D.C., Baltimore, Philadelphia and New York City. In the eastern half of the U.S., heroin has mainly been available in powder form rather than the black tar heroin more common in the west. It is easier to mix fentanyl with powdered heroin. In a 12-month period ending at the end of April 2021, some 100,306 died in the U.S., up 28.5 percent over the same period a year earlier.

In February 2023 US Congressman Dan Newhouse claimed China is responsible for over 90 percent of illicit fentanyl found in the United States. "We simply cannot allow the lethal fentanyl engine in China to run while communities are being torn apart. We simply cannot trust them to be a responsible stakeholder and address this crisis in good faith."

In May 2022 the Council on Foreign Relations reported that since 2000 more than a million people in the United States have died of drug overdoses, the majority of which were due to opioids. Millions more Americans suffer from opioid addiction. Many health experts attribute the high death toll to what they say was years of overprescribing by physicians. Doctors began prescribing more opioids amid a growing concern that pain was going undertreated, and also because pharmaceutical companies began marketing the drugs more aggressively while claiming they posed little risk.

Health-care providers reported feeling pressure to prescribe opioid medications rather than alternatives, such as physical therapy or acupuncture, because patients request them and other treatments are often more costly or less accessible. "We didn't develop an opioid epidemic until there was a huge surplus of opioids, which started with pharmaceutical drugs distributed legally," New York Special Narcotics Prosecutor Bridget G. Brennan.

The vast majority of those who overdose on opioids are non-Hispanic white Americans, who made up close to 70 percent of the annual total in

2020. Black Americans and Hispanic Americans accounted for about 17 and 12 percent of cases, respectively. Economists Anne Case and Angus Deaton have argued that the rise in what they call "deaths of despair"— which include drug overdoses, particularly among white Americans without college degrees—is primarily the result of wages stagnating over the last four decades and a decline in available jobs. U.S. military veterans, many of whom suffer from chronic pain as a result of their service, account for a disproportionately high number of opioid-related deaths. Veterans are twice as likely as the general population to die from an opioid overdose, according to a study commissioned by the National Institutes of Health.

Opioids have also taken a toll on the economy. The Center for Disease Control calculates that opioid misuse costs the country some $78 billion per year, a tally that includes costs from health care, lost productivity, treatment programs, and legal expenses. In 2017 alone, the cost of opioid misuse and fatal overdoses was estimated to be around $1 trillion. Testifying before the U.S. Senate in 2017, Treasury Secretary Janet Yellen, then chair of the Federal Reserve, linked the opioid epidemic to declining labor-force participation among "prime-age workers."

CHINA

According to National Public Radio, for drug traffickers interested in getting in on the fentanyl business, all roads once led to Wuhan, China. The sprawling industrial city built along the Yangtze River in east-central China is known for its production of chemicals, including the ingredients needed to cook fentanyl and other powerful synthetic opioids. Vendors there shipped huge quantities around the world. The biggest customers were Mexican drug cartels, which have embraced fentanyl in recent years because it is cheaper and easier to produce than heroin.

But the COVID pandemic that emerged in Wuhan before spreading across the planet disrupted the fentanyl supply chain, causing a ripple effect that cut into the profits of Mexican traffickers and drove up street drug prices across the United States. Chinese vendors are often camouflaged by a complex network of corporate entities registered in far-flung cities along China's interior, where they use sophisticated shipping methods to bypass screening measures and where law enforcement scrutiny is often laxer than in bigger cities such as Beijing or Shanghai.

A salesperson for Hebei Aicrowe Biotech Co. Ltd., a pharmaceuticals maker registered in Shijiazhuang, the capital of Hebei province, said the company had drastically reduced the number of synthetic opioids and other compounds it offered because of the heightened legal scrutiny in China. But when NPR visited the company the salesperson confirmed it still sold "99918," which is code for a popular fentanyl precursor, banned in China in 2018. "The customer has the responsibility to guarantee the compound is legal where the receiving address is," the salesperson said.

Fentanyl production and exports continue apace in obscure Chinese cities. Synthetic opioid vendors favor working out of China's industrial hinterlands, where policing can be less strict. China has a vast pharmaceuticals and bulk chemical manufacturing sector, making compounds sold globally intended for legitimate purposes in medicine and industrial processes. Synthetic opioid vendors shield themselves behind layers of interlinked companies registered in these sectors or related fields such as biotechnology. The drug vendors NPR visited worked out of offices tucked away in shopping malls, residential towers and industrial complexes.

Vendors continue to operate openly on platforms, including Facebook, Twitter, Wickr, MeWe and Vimeo, advertising a head-spinning array of chemicals tagged with an obscure but internationally used numerical naming system. Sellers and buyers know the obscure acronyms, code names, chemical registration numbers and the like, and are able to change on a dime when one trusted member of a group is raided or arrested. U.S. law enforcement acknowledged struggling to curb this online fentanyl marketplace, in part because many of the transactions are encrypted. Louise Shelley, a George Mason University professor who researches fentanyl supply chains and studied the impact of the pandemic on sales said. "The problem has not ended. [Fentanyl sales] are still going on the open Web."

Analysts said an entire new class of synthetic opioids – a family of compounds called benzimidazoles – is now showing up in U.S. drug busts and leading to overdose deaths. The drugs are completely different in chemical structure from fentanyl, but experts warn they can be just as deadly. Initial seizures of the drugs come from mailed packages originating in China, where their production is not controlled. China and other countries often turn the tables on the US and blame Americans for the addiction problem which drives the demand. It's not as simple as saying, 'China, stop producing and exporting these chemicals'. There are several sides to this issue. In response, China, for example, could counter with: 'Americans, stop buying and using drugs.'

Index

BIBLIOGRAPHY
(SELECTED)

Cooper, Sam, *Wilful Blindness: How a network of narcos, tycoons and CCP agents infiltrated the West (Holding the Chinese Communist Party to Account)*, Ottawa: Optima Publishing, 2021.

Hébert, Jaques, *Two Innocents in Red China*, Oxford: Oxford University Press, 1968.

Holt, Tate, *Yamashita's Gold*, San Francisco: Berkeley Hills Book, 1998.

Homer-Dixon, Thomas, *Commanding Hope: The Power We Have to Renew a World in Peril*, Toronto: Vintage Canada, 2022.

Manthorpe, Jonathan, *Claws of the Panda: Beijing's Campaign of Influence and Intimidation in Canada*, Toronto: Cormorant Books, 2019.

Matthiessen, Peter and Iyer, Pico *Snow Leopard, The*, New York, Penguin Classics, 2008.

Nutter, John Jacob, *CIA's Black Ops: Covert Action, Foreign Policy, and Democracy, The*, Buffalo: Prometheus, 1999.

Seagrave, Sterling and Seagrave, Peggy, *Gold Warriors: America's Secret Recovery of Yamashita's Gold*, London: Verso Books, 2005.

Seagrave, Sterling and Seagrave, Peggy,, *The Yamato Dynasty: The Secret History of Japan's Imperial Family*, New York: Broadway, 2000.

Schaller, George B., *Stones of Silence: Journeys in the Himalayas*, New York: Bantam, 1982.

Sutton, Antony, *America's Secret Establishment: An Introduction to the Order of Skull & Bones*, Walterville: TrineDay, 2003.

Winchester, Simon, *River at the Center of the World: A Journey Up the Yangtze, and Back in Chinese Time, The*, London: Picador, 2004..

MICHAEL McCARTHY TRAVEL BOOKS AVAILABLE ON AMAZON

(Google the phrase "Amazon travel books Michael McCarthy" to locate any of these books)

Halfway to Heaven in Huatulco: Finding Paradise in Southern Mexico
Softcover, 150 pages, colour photos   Coming 2023

The Snow Leopard Returns: Tracking Peter Matthiessen to Crystal Mountain and beyond
Softcover, adventure, b&w photos

In the Shadow of the Iguana: Looking for the legacy of John Huston in Puerto Vallarta
Softcover, adventure travel, history and biography, guide to Puerto Vallarta, full colour

London Calling: Finding Jack London in the Valley of the Moon
Softcover, adventure travel, biography, explanations of synchronicity

Amazing Adventures #1!
Softcover, travel humour, full colour photos

Amazing Adventures #2
Softcover, travel humour, b&w photos

Better than Snarge: Trips Gone Wrong, Poor Decisions Along the Way and Mighty Adventures in Faraway Places
Softcover, text with b&w photos, travel humour, no photos

Negotiating India: Never Drive In Countries Where They Believe in Reincarnation
Softcover, travel humour, adventure, b&w photos

Portraits of People and the Places They Live
Coffee table photobook, full colour, 750 photos with supporting text

Into the Great Bear: Searching for the Spirit Bear in the World's Last Remaining Temperate Rainforest
Softcover, adventure travel, full colour photos, guidebook

Transformative Travels: How to Change the World on Your Journey through life
Softcover, text with b&w photos, guidebook for micro-philanthropic travel

Tracking Jack: Following Kerouac to Desolation Peak
Softcover, travel, coffee table book format, full colour

Forever Young: How to Re-invent Yourself in Times of Constant Change
Softcover, biography (Frank Ogden) text with b&w photos